"Treating people with fairness and respect at work is the very cornerstone of a positive employee experience. Hanna Hasl-Kelchner doesn't just explain it in *Seeking Fairness at Work*, she provides a common-sense framework for doing so, one based on solid research. People managers at all levels should buy and read this book."

Barbara Mitchell & Cornelia Gamlem, authors of *The Big Book of HR*

"A must-read for senior leaders. Hasl-Kelchner deconstructs the social contract that drives employee engagement and excellence, identifies common pitfalls, and provides a 5-step strategy for building fairness and trust at work. It's like she reads your mind by articulating the concerns you might have about following the steps, then without invalidating that point of view, she manages to shift your perspective. Hasl-Kelchner is a master at the human relationships that are the foundation of any workplace. If you want your employees to bring their full commitment and best ideas to work, read *Seeking Fairness at Work*."

Rusty Gaillard, team performance and leadership excellence consultant, best-selling author of *Breaking the Code*

"It's not fair! The lament every leader ought to dread. Because the minute someone feels like they've been short-changed, they feel entitled to take. Unfairness is one of the greatest predictors of dishonesty. Fortunately, Hanna Hasl-Kelchner has provided us a roadmap for how to make sure our workplaces and teams cultivate this universal value we all hunger for. If you want a level playing field where everyone on your team can thrive, take Hanna's well-crafted advice to heart. You'll be so glad you did."

Ron Carucci, Managing Partner, Navalent, best-selling and award-winning author of *Rising to Power* and *To Be Honest*

"Long before I ran a company, I worked for several as an employee. Back then, constructs like trust, accountability, and fairness at work were mere whispers. Today, employees have digital megaphones. *Seeking Fairness at Work* is a masterful strategy for leaders balancing empathy, engagement, and execution in the modern workplace."

Olalah Njenga, CEO, YellowWood Group LLC and Vice Chair, NCWorks Commission

"Fairness in the workplace is a critical yet elusive concept for most managers and organizations. In this book, Hanna Hasl-Kelchner thoroughly breaks down the concept and provides up-to-date guidance on how to manage effectively and fairly, anchored by relevant examples and her helpful Fairness Factors. I recommend it to anyone who is looking for a truly useful resource on ethical people management."

Rob Wood, Managing Attorney – Operations, Soule Employment Law Firm

"Hanna has done us all a favor by writing this book. She has significantly added value for all of us who are wanting a better workplace environment. By focusing on what's fair as her foundational element she moves us through a process of determining how to do it better. She shows us how to rebuild trust, improve relationship chemistry, and find genuine accountability—all critically important to building and sustaining a strong people-centered culture. Finally, the discussion on a cultural and structural safety net is necessary for a comprehensive workplace understanding. For all of us who are interested in understanding, creating, and maintaining a strong, employee-based culture, this is a must-read."

Warren Rustand, CEO, Summit Capital Consulting LLC

"Hanna has unique compassion for understanding the basics of employee fairness and cultures that provide the right things for them to thrive. She is brave in her assessment of both the barriers and breakthroughs and speaks wonderfully from the point of view of employees at all levels of an organization. I hope managers, leaders, and executives take the time to read, internalize, and exercise the wealth of information and guidance she provides the reader. The right advice; at just the right time."

Jim Jeffers, CEO, HRrenewal®

"The pre-pandemic leadership models do not work with today's generation of workers. Employees have changed their mindsets about the role of work and the workplace. It's time that leaders do as well. *Seeking Fairness at Work* lays out a usable playbook for leaders on the important aspects of leading people they need to employ to create workplaces of wellbeing and safety. Following the advice in this book will lead to desired results. Anyone who ignores this advice will shorten their leadership career."

Steven Howard, author and leadership mentor, Humony Leadership

"One of the most interesting studies I ever read showed that the very best small businesses had one thing in common. Was it great marketing? No. A great location? No again. A superior product? Nope. It was that they were all run by great managers. Turns out great managers foster happy employees, and happy employees create repeat customers. Hanna Hasl-Kelchner's new book, *Seeking Fairness at Work*, shows how any leader can be the type of leader that makes a difference. Highly recommended!"

Steve Strauss, best-selling author and *Inc. Magazine* columnist

"What sets this book apart is its holistic approach to leadership. It's not just a guide to becoming a better leader; it's a call to action for those looking to make a real difference in the world around them. It's for the aspiring leaders who influence through action rather than words, the servant leaders who put the needs of their team above their own, and the conscious leaders who lead with awareness and intentionality. *Seeking Fairness at Work* is a must-read for anyone committed to fostering a leadership style that is effective and deeply human."

Cheryl Johnson, Performance Solution Specialist, The Fifth Principle Learning Cooperative

Seeking

Fairness

at Work

Cracking the New Code of Greater Employee Engagement, Retention & Satisfaction

• • •

H. HASL-KELCHNER, MBA, JD

SMART DIRECTION PRESS
div. of Business M.O., LLC

Other Books Authored or Co-Authored by Hanna Hasl-Kelchner

The Business Guide to Legal Literacy

Champions: Knockout Strategies for Health, Wealth and Success

Published by Smart Direction Press, Research Triangle Park, NC; a division of Business M.O., LLC.

Smart Directions Press publishes its books in a variety of formats. Some content that appears in print may not be available in electronic books.

Readers should be aware that Internet links offered as citations and/or sources for further information may have changed or disappeared between the time this was written and when it is read.

ISBN: 979-8990029-1-0

Library of Congress Control Number: 2024906853

This book is dedicated

To the courageous executives, managers, and entrepreneurs committed to raising their employees' game instead of their defenses;

To the HR professionals, employment attorneys, training and coaching professionals, and the networking and trade associations whose important work nurtures and empowers the health of their members' and clients' business culture; and

To the employees experiencing a sense of injustice in the workplace who want to restore their self-confidence.

This book is for you.

TABLE OF CONTENTS

For Marta, a pharmaceutical sales representative, the final straw was being reprimanded for not responding to her boss' email while on vacation, even though she told him she'd have no Internet access. After logging in 80-hour weeks the previous months to successfully launch a new product, Marta believed she had earned some much-needed rest. Having her personal boundary ignored over something a colleague later told her wasn't urgent made Marta realize how her private time was being disrespected and her contributions taken for granted.

For Omar, a mid-level information technology director, the "aha" moment came when he recognized there was nothing his manager, an executive vice president, could say or do anymore to restore trust in their working relationship. It was bad enough when the manager continuously embarrassed Omar in department meetings by cutting him off mid-sentence and trivializing his work while colleagues with similar responsibilities were allowed to drone on in detail. When his supervisor openly humiliated him in the boardroom, in front of senior management, treating him like a gofer, something deep inside Omar said, "Enough."

For Will, a financial services manager, the breaking point came when he heard his supervisor say, "Everybody in business lies" while bragging about a large business deal he had just signed. It made Will realize his boss could lie about anything, including performance reviews. The lack of honesty presented an ethical dilemma and a risk Will was no longer prepared to take.

And then there's Mary, a senior data analyst for a consumer products company. Her employer gladly embraced remote work arrangements during the COVID-19 pandemic, and she was told she could live anywhere provided she had a reliable Internet connection and could participate in weekly department Zoom calls held on Pacific time. Mary was grateful for the flexibility. Another department manager had been making unwelcome sexual advances and working remotely let her avoid him. Besides, her husband had just retired and her new freedom allowed them to sell their house and move to their dream home deep in the wine country, two hours further away from the office drama.

But three years later, her boss reneged on the remote arrangement, even though her work performance was exemplary. A companywide return to office policy went into effect, requiring her to be in the office five days a week or to find another job. Mary was torn by the news and felt betrayed, especially since she was only a few years away from retirement herself and leaving early meant sacrificing certain company benefits. She ultimately bit the bullet and resigned.

Perhaps you know someone like Will, Marta, Omar, Mary, or perhaps you *are* one of them. They're all solid performers, dedicated employees, and respected colleagues. No one expected them to give notice, least of all their bosses.

Employees have been reevaluating their life, clarifying priorities, and reexamining their careers for more than ten years according to research by Harvard Business School professors, Joseph Fuller and William Kerr, and that trend is here to stay they say. Employees are looking for a better way to live. They want more flexibility and autonomy.

Fairness at work is something employees expect and managers genuinely believe they're delivering. But low employee engagement rates reported by Gallup's annual State of the Global Workplace Reports say otherwise. Their 2023 Report estimates it represents an $8.8 trillion global problem. And the biggest source of employee discontent and unease cited in the report? Unfair treatment at work.

The overall tolerance for unfair treatment has diminished due to a number of changing community standards, namely:

- the War for Talent amid the coming of age of two large workforce cohorts (Millennials and Gen X) that research says have different workplace needs than their predecessors and whose sheer size affords them the extraordinary market power of demanding change and rejecting command-and-control leadership;

- the #MeToo movement that mandates accountability from organizations for employees who use positional power to sexually harass and extort others in the workplace; and

- the Black Lives Matter (#BLM) movement whose social justice mission spills into the workplace with calls for more diversity along with meaningful inclusion and equity to counterbalance structural inequalities.

Employees have moved the high cost of unfairness at work into the "unacceptable" column on their emotional balance sheet. Evidence includes the growing visibility of employees "quiet quitting" and the Great Resignation spawned by the COVID pandemic where employees simply refuse to accept the intolerable anymore. Indeed, these changes in the labor market have permanently altered the very meaning of work, leaving organizations scrambling to catch up.

Fairness Matters

Fairness is a universal human value that transcends cultures around the world. Unfairness at work is demoralizing and is an especially toxic stressor because it attacks us personally according to Dr. E. Kevin Kelloway, Canada Research Chair in Occupational Health Psychology at Saint Mary's University. It's an affront to our dignity and core identity. And, as a toxic stressor, it's impact can be felt far beyond momentary emotional stress and lead to serious physical symptoms. It attacks who we are, and when we're under assault, our bodies get flooded with adrenaline and stress hormones such as cortisol.

Cortisol can wreak serious havoc. If we suddenly find ourselves experiencing frequent upset stomachs that our doctor later concludes is acid reflux, we can probably thank cortisol. Experiencing weight gain?

We probably can thank cortisol for that one too. Its impact is felt on our thyroid gland where it slows down our metabolism and on our adrenal glands where it can increase our hunger. Comfort foods high in fat and sugar content can temporarily make us feel better but tip the scales in an unhealthy direction. Cortisol's impact on the adrenal glands can also decrease our appetite for sex. So, between unhealthy weight gain and strained personal relationships it's common to feel depressed. Stress can even affect the body at the cellular level, weathering us from the inside out and contributing to premature signs of aging. Great, huh?

Weekends provide a welcome respite from workplace stress and opportunity to recharge. But the relief is short-lived. On Sunday afternoon our stomachs are in knots as we steel ourselves for the work week ahead. It's a phenomenon dubbed the "Sunday Scaries," and a survey commissioned by LinkedIn, the world's largest professional online network, discovered 80% of working adults experience it. So, while we may not be alone in suffering, it's a soul-crushing club we didn't particularly want to join; but one we may feel stuck in. It's no wonder employee engagement rates fluctuate within narrow bands in Gallup reports and surveys from year to year.

The Value of High Employee Engagement

Definitions of employee engagement vary depending on the source. The central idea is that when workers feel fairly supported to do their best work, when they are included and feel like they belong, they bring an extra degree of energy and discretionary effort to the table because they're more emotionally and intellectually committed. What *they* do matters. They matter. Their commitment to the organization therefore goes far beyond just showing up for work and robotically meeting job requirements in exchange for a paycheck. They feel empowered and inspired to go above and beyond the call of duty.

Employee engagement is incredibly powerful. Organizations vigorously pursue it because research shows those with a highly engaged workforce experience:

- 2.6 times higher earnings-per-share,

- double the net income,
- seven times greater 5-year total annual shareholder return,
- 19.2% higher growth in annual operating income,
- triple the profit growth compared to competitors,
- double the customer loyalty and employee productivity; and
- 87% less employee attrition.

Those are impressive numbers.

The Huge Cost of Low Employee Engagement

In contrast, and in addition to the physical and emotional cost to employees on both sides of the desk, organizations with low employee engagement miss out on its benefits *and* get penalized with 37% more absenteeism and lost productivity. Gallup estimates it costs employers $3,400 for every $10,000 a disengaged employee earns. In other words, it's a productivity penalty of 34% of their annual pay. Multiply that by the number of disengaged employees on a payroll, and the out-of-pocket opportunity cost adds up fast.

There is also a high correlation between employee engagement and retention. Research shows that there is a 48% chance that employees with low engagement will quit, making it a gateway to employee turnover. While managers may be willing to take that risk, believing they could reclaim some lost productivity with eager new hires, the reality isn't so rosy. Organizations are really swapping a large expense for an even *bigger* one.

The hiring and training cost of replacing an employee is between 30–50% of their annual salary at the entry level and up to 400% at the most senior ranks. What makes that turnover price tag deceptive is how it fails to include collateral damage resulting from coworkers who now have to work harder and longer in the interim, with the extra workload potentially contributing to their burnout. It also ignores the loss of valuable information, such as institutional knowledge when long-term employees leave, or the potential loss of proprietary information (absent a confidentiality agreement).

Other costs include hiccups in established business relationships when a customer-facing employee quits and lost revenue if they're able to transition customers to their new employer or start-up. Departing employees can also inspire those left behind to start looking for new positions, causing an even bigger exodus.

Worst of all is how employee churn destabilizes business operations. It keeps teams from gelling. It distracts leadership with a continuous recruiting process. It compromises the remaining employees' willingness and ability to learn new things because they're strapped for time doing extra work, and it kills momentum by chewing up resources that could otherwise be spent moving the business forward.

Meanwhile, disengaged employees who stay on the payroll can infect the organization's culture with their halfhearted approach and hamper performance because they're more likely to miss deadlines, goals, and sales targets. They also contribute to increased customer complaints and workers' compensation, harassment, and discrimination claims, and keep potential legal problems buried until they're too big to hide, at which point they're also more expensive to fix.

It gets potentially worse when employee dissatisfaction stems from mismanagement of a legal or an ethical issue, turning disgruntled workers into whistleblowers. Public disclosures can cause a firestorm of unwanted media attention, creating legal liability and reputation damage for individual managers and the organization as a whole.

Yet one of the most overlooked and distressing disengagement landmines is the connection to workplace violence. Disengaged employees are more likely to feel more stressed, worried, and angrier than their engaged peers. It sets the stage for conflict that can easily spill into threatening behaviors such as bullying, harassment, retaliation, or physical altercations.

Altogether, the financial and psychological toll of low employee engagement on the workplace is enormous.

The Urgent Need for Change
Evolving employee priorities are colliding with traditional command-

and-control style management that tends to view hiring its workforce transactionally, managing them with positional power and an emphasis on bottom-line metrics, rather than people-focused, relationship-building strategies. Simply put: old-school management isn't meeting new-school needs. It's a standoff that won't improve until managers understand *why* employees respond negatively to workplace culture and appreciate *how* low employee engagement, satisfaction, and retention are *symptoms* of a suboptimal culture, one that management controls and can change.

Leadership matters. Workers change jobs because they leave their manager, not the company. Indeed, the quality of supervisory personnel is the single biggest factor in job change decisions according to the book *It's the Manager*. Other research finds 75% of employees think their direct manager is the most stressful part of the job, and 65% say they'd rather have a new manager than a pay raise.

Ouch!

It's against this backdrop of workplace discontent, including a staggering 59% of workers being disengaged, or "quiet quitting" in Gallup's 2023 parlance, and another 18% being actively disengaged, or just plain miserable at work and "loud quitting," that *Seeking Fairness at Work* begins.

As a business strategist and attorney, frustrated employees have shared their feelings of helplessness and anger with me many times over the years. They were upset about the organization's willful blindness to management behaviors that torched their dignity, confidence, and psychological safety. When raising a serious issue about the behavior of a senior vice president with the head of human resources at a large manufacturing company, for example, an employee was essentially shooed away. "It's worse in other departments," they were told. In desperation, they consulted a lawyer.

This story is but a small sample of the misguided leadership behaviors I've witnessed over the years that damage trust and result in unintended negative consequences. No, they didn't always trigger lawsuits. Although, many could have. But they were always costly in terms of diminished employee engagement, retention, and definitely satisfaction.

Book Overview

The goal of *Seeking Fairness at Work* is to help employees recognize they are not alone in feeling frustrated at work and that their expectations of fairness are reasonable. The chapters ahead give voice to their stories, with names changed to protect their privacy.

But even more important than providing solace to workers, by sharing the employee perspective, *Seeking Fairness at Work* offers managers a roadmap for change by giving them a clear-eyed view of the cultural norms in their organization that nobody wants to talk about, an explanation of why they may not realize how off-putting those behaviors are, and why the imbalance of power in the employee-employer relationship puts the onus on them to take the lead in addressing fairness at work by delivering on implied social contract inherent in every employee-employer relationship.

Even though leadership and management are different from a technical standpoint, I use them interchangeably throughout the book because they both share a common need to get work done through others, to influence and motivate them; and both leaders and managers find themselves struggling with how to inspire more employee commitment and productivity.

Cracking the new code of employee engagement, retention, and satisfaction requires an understanding of how unfairness at work is experienced by employees. It's impossible to solve a problem without understanding it's dimensions and scope. That's why this book begins with Part 1: What Employees Secretly Wish They Could Tell Their Boss About Unfairness at Work *(And What Bosses Really Need to Hear)*.

Chapter 1: What's Fair describes the legal and psychological justification for expectations of fairness at work: the covenants of good faith and fair dealing required by the implied social contract and the human motivational needs identified by Abraham Maslow.

Chapter 2: The Workplace Norms Nobody Wants to Talk About delves into the most common unwritten workplace rules that determine how organizations really operate, how those norms represent a behavioral continuum ranging from small management indiscretions to the more egregious, and why they crush high employee engagement.

Chapter 3: How Power Changes Everything examines why management is often unaware and less empathetic to employee needs and may not realize how their acts and omissions cumulatively contribute to perceptions of unfairness at work.

> *"We cannot solve problems with the same thinking*
> *we used when we created them."*
> ~Albert Einstein

Part 2: A Five-Part Strategy for Improving Fairness at Work offers an integrated, multipronged approach to instilling more good faith and fair dealing into the organization's culture to help raise employees' game instead of their defenses.

Chapter 4: Restore Employee Trust with More Self-Awareness details the benefit to management of being mindful of their how their behaviors affect others and influence trust. It also explores why employee engagement and satisfaction surveys are rarely a one-size-fits-

all solution to rebuilding trust and improving employee engagement, satisfaction, and retention.

Genuine empathy can help leaders put more self-awareness into action, but it's often thought of as a single, monolithic thing, and that's why **Chapter 5: Improve Relationship Chemistry with More Empathy** makes empathy more visible by breaking it down into elements that bring positive energy into the room. It thereby makes it easier for managers to demonstrate fairness and build the kind of trust that makes saying "I'm sorry" or "That's not what I meant" believable.

Nothing says fairness like accountability and **Chapter 6: Make Genuine Accountability a Cornerstone** shows how honest and consistent conflict management processes and skills are essential to bringing errant behavior back in line at *all* levels of the organization. It also shows how accountability creates guard rails to ensure that employee recognition and getting ahead is based on merit, not things beyond their control.

Accountability, similar to any other management responsibility, is only as effective as the skillset and mindset of the people carrying out those tasks because keeping the enemies at the gate is what helps organizations **Maintain a Cultural Safety Net** (Chapter 7). It requires rigorous processes and safeguards to ensure that those operating at the frontlines of employee satisfaction, engagement, and retention have the tools necessary to responsibly manage the human capital they're entrusted with.

Last, but not least, **Chapter 8: Mend the Structural Safety Net**, directs attention to the organization's governance documents, the vision and mission statements, and the policies, procedures, guidelines, and job descriptions that formally manage employee expectations. A strong structural safety net provides consistency and reliability, allowing leaders to sidestep *ad hoc* decisions that can be perceived as unfair, especially around accountability and conflict management.

Over one hundred **Fairness Factors** are included in the following chapters to improve awareness and highlight incremental opportunities for management to unlock the cultural potential of their organization, that wealth of dormant creativity and productivity already on the payroll.

This doesn't sound like how things are "supposed" to work is what some managers may think out loud.

I hear you. The concepts in this book can challenge assumptions of how things are "supposed" to work in employment relationships. They may surface concerns and fears we may not even realize we have. That's why I honor that little voice in our heads and *express those thoughts in italics* throughout the text because those are conversations that need to be had and the misunderstandings that need to be addressed.

Altogether, *Seeking Fairness at Work* challenges employer "truths" and offers a new perspective on employee engagement by reframing it as a *response* to how power is used in the workplace and how power causes leaders to miss solutions hiding in plain view.

My hope for employees reading this book is that they find comfort in knowing their expectations of fairness at work are reasonable and justified.

For executives, managers, and entrepreneurs reading this book, my hope is (1) they acquire a new appreciation for their employees' experiences and what it means for their duty of good asset stewardship; (2) gain a deeper understanding of why certain past efforts to improve employee satisfaction, engagement, and retention have been suboptimal and (3) discover why a synchronized five-part strategy focused on the implied social contract that makes the covenants of good faith and fair dealing a central goal is a management lodestar.

With the War for Talent hotter than ever before, smoothing over those speed bumps and facilitating management's ability to demonstrate good faith and fair dealing creates an unparalleled competitive edge.

With more fairness at work, everyone wins.

Part

One

What Employees Secretly Wish They Could Tell Their Boss About Unfairness at Work

(And What Bosses Really Need to Hear)

Chapter 1

What's Fair?

Fairness is a universal human value that transcends cultures around the world. As children we understand the concept implicitly. When kids want to join a new game on the playground, they ask, "How do you play," and rightly so. They want to know the rules: what's expected of them, what they can expect from others, and what to expect as an outcome. They want to know how they should relate to one another to move the ball forward, reach the goal, and score the points. After all, who doesn't want to advance? To win? Nobody.

It doesn't take long for them to figure out who plays by the rules, who doesn't, and who makes it up as they go along. When expectations are unmet or become moving targets, indignant howls of "That's not fair" and accusations of "cheater" quickly fill the air. When the foul is particularly egregious or continuous, the game is no fun anymore. Kids take their ball and go home. Simple.

The grown-up version in the workplace follows a similar emotional arc but differs in important ways. Employees are never more engaged at work than on their first day at a new job. With fresh opportunities comes hope. With hope comes excitement, enthusiasm, and a touch of trepidation because nobody wants to offend the higher-ups by breaking an unwritten rule. New hires are on high alert.

It can take weeks, months, and even years for employees to figure out how things really work in an organization. And when they do, they may be reluctant to call out any improprieties they discover. The workplace is a different ball game. Temper tantrums and name calling can swiftly ruin someone's reputation and unceremoniously get them fired. Besides, maturity makes employees more resilient.

But just because adults have thicker skin doesn't mean they lose their ability to recognize unfairness or experience it. The hurt can still run deep. They take their ball home differently when encountering unreasonable situations. They'll push back against unfairness by being less emotionally present, by exploiting attendance or time-off policies, arriving to work late, leaving early, surfing the Internet for personal use on company time, not taking initiative, and/or doing the minimum.

The Real Deal About Fairness

Every employment relationship carries with it certain expectations of fairness. Employees give up a huge chunk of their time every week in service to employers, spending more time at work than with their loved ones. As a result, they want more than a paycheck in exchange for their time and talent. Employees want their work to matter, to be personally treated with respect, and management's support to do their job.

OK, what exactly does that mean?

It's simple: employees want a number of things, including a sense of belonging.

―――― FAIRNESS FACTOR ――――
Fairness is about belonging.

But they DO belong . . . they're on the payroll.

Money is good. But it's not enough. Employees want something more. They want to be seen. They want to be respected. They want to be to be included and accepted as human beings in something bigger than themselves, not treated as modern-day chattel.

―――― FAIRNESS FACTOR ――――
Fairness is about esteem.

Belonging and the psychological needs it represents are substantial non-monetary components of employee compensation. It's about being part of a community and having contributions be recognized and appropriately rewarded. It's about connection and overall support that goes beyond mere financial rewards.

What all this means for employers is if monetary remuneration is x, belonging and inclusion turns the employee experience into x+.

Well, hey that's great, but management has expectations too, you know.

Indeed. Management wants something more in exchange for the wages they pay, too. They want all the intangibles associated with high employee engagement. They want enthusiasm, loyalty, creativity, initiative, innovation, and, of course, high productivity. They want employees' full commitment to move the business forward.

What that means for employees is if coming to work on time and adhering to job requirements is y, full employee engagement turns their labor into y+ for management.

Combining the implied expectations of employees and employers creates the social contract. It can be summed up as follows in Figure 1.1 below.

THE SOCIAL CONTRACT

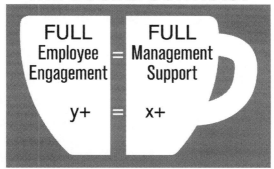

FULL Employee Engagement	=	FULL Management Support
y+	=	x+

Figure 1.1

When the social contract is expressly discussed and clearly understood, it can be the foundation of great success. Everyone puts all their cards on the table. No hidden aces. No surprises. The transparency it creates is what lawyers call a "meeting of the minds," a common understanding of "this is what we're each going do to achieve a common goal."

Some organizations claim they commit their workplace social contract to writing. They believe having new hires sign such documents cements positive behaviors and encourages a culture of trust, respect, accountability, and achievement. Sadly, very few companies engage in this practice.

But just because a social contract isn't written doesn't mean it fails to exist. It's still there. Only now, it's implied. It arises from the very existence of the employment arrangement because people don't stop having reasonable expectations.

Everyone has their own beliefs about how things *should* work in the employment relationship. But implied agreements are treacherous turf by their very nature because people make assumptions when things aren't spelled out. This creates fertile ground for misunderstanding and disappointment. And that's where the fun begins.

Wait a minute . . . how can these hidden expectations be so powerful? What right does anyone have to those beliefs in the first place, when the employer gets to set the rules? What could possibly be the basis of any employee expectations in this implied social contract?

Excellent questions.

The Implied Covenants of Good Faith and Fair Dealing

To help understand why the failure to appreciate the role of the social contract can land such a profound emotional blow to employee engagement it's important to note that every agreement carries with it an inescapable obligation of good faith and fair dealing—even implied agreements. This legalese basically means both parties need to "play nice." The parties need to be faithful to the scope, purpose, and terms of the employee-employer relationship. Another way to think of it is to adhere to community standards of decency, fairness, or reasonableness. These are obligations that cannot be waived.

FAIRNESS FACTOR

Fairness is about acting in good faith and with fair dealing.

It should be noted that this good faith covenant is *not* to be confused with the duty of good faith associated with a fiduciary relationship. It's different. A fiduciary is required to put the best interests of the beneficiary first. It exists, for example, in relationships between attorneys and their clients, or between guardians and their wards. That's not the case in an employee-employer arrangement.

Even though workers receive compensation, they are not beneficiaries in a legal sense. As a result, employers are not required to put employees' best interests first. But that doesn't mean those interests should be ignored. Employers do so at their peril.

Good faith in the context of an employee-employer relationship requires honesty in the contract performance. Honest compensation and safe working conditions are two examples.

───── ┤ **FAIRNESS FACTOR** ├ ─────
Fairness is about honest compensation and safe working conditions.

Taking advantage of employees by short-changing these needs is not only unfair, it's also highly demotivating and diminishes trust. Good faith corresponds with the most basic human motivational needs identified by Abraham Maslow in his 1943 paper "A Theory of Human Motivation": the need for physical safety and the physiological necessities of food, water, and shelter. After all, it is only through honest compensation and safe working conditions that we're able to satisfy those basic physiological needs. That's why it's highly demotivating when working conditions fall short on this front, and it should come as no surprise to management that employee satisfaction dwindles.

The findings of Maslow's seminal paper, often referred to as Maslow's Hierarchy of Human Motivational Needs, is a roadmap of performance incentives and dovetails with the covenants of good faith and fair dealing. When viewed in tandem they're highly instructive on how to boost employee engagement.

Maslow's basic needs, for example, can be said to represent employees' minimum expectations, the x in the $y+ = x+$ equation. Those fundamental requirements, as previously noted, which align with the covenant of good faith are detailed in the bottom row of Figure 1.2 below, How Compliance with Covenants of Good Faith and Fair Dealing Align with Maslow's Hierarchy and Influence Employee Engagement.

PSYCHOLOGICAL CONTRACT	MASLOW'S HIERARCHY		EMPLOYEE ENGAGEMENT
FAIR DEALING Requires fair and honest non-monetary compensation. The need that neither party will do anything to destroy or injure the right of the other party to receive the benefits of the contract.	*PSYCHOLOGICAL NEEDS* *(X+)*	*ESTEEM* prestige, sense of accomplishment *BELONGING* relationship/sense of community be seen /connect / support	
GOOD FAITH Honest monetary compensation & working conditions.	*BASIC NEEDS* *(X)*	*SAFETY* security, safety *PHYSIOLOGICAL* food, water, warmth, rest	

Figure 1.2 How Compliance with Covenants of Good Faith and Fair Dealing Align with Maslow's Hierarchy and Influence Employee Engagement

Minimum good faith working conditions yield minimum employee engagement. To transform the employee experience from x into x+ and unlock more employee engagement requires fair dealing. It's about management providing *reasonable* support to employees so they can do their job.

FAIRNESS FACTOR

Fairness is about providing employees with reasonable support,
so they can do their jobs.

It would be unfair, for example, to punish employees if management were to unreasonably fail to cooperate or provide reasonable support. Under those circumstances the non-performance under the implied contract would, in legal parlance, be excused.

In Maslow's world fair dealing translates into meeting the employees' psychological needs of esteem and belonging. Research from BetterUp Labs finds that a sense of belonging is both motivational and financially rewarding. More specifically, it learned that if a 10,000-employee workforce experienced a high degree of belonging, it would correlate to an annual increase productivity of more than $52 million. On the other hand, when employees experience exclusion, they participate less.

Diminished collaboration should come as no surprise. After all, if someone feels isolated, are they the first person to raise their hand

and volunteer new ideas? Do they jump in and happily advance a conversation? Of course not. They're too afraid of taking that risk because they've already been treated as "other." BetterUp also discovered that employees who did not have a sense of belonging at work suffered from 158% more anxiety and depression, 109% more burnout, and 77% more stress than their more engaged peers.

Some of the employee expectations identified in Figure 1.2 have been codified by law, turning them into legal rights. These include fair labor laws that set minimum wage standards, occupational safety laws designed to protect the physical well-being of workers, the Universal Declaration of Human Rights adopted by the United Nations General Assembly in 1948 that mirrors Maslow's basic physiological needs of food, water, shelter and clothing in Article 25, and the psychological needs of belonging and sense of connection in Article 16. Unfortunately, some managers don't know what the law requires in their specific jurisdiction. As a result, they're blissfully unaware of how they could be violating it.

"Low Employee Engagement" Dilemma

Employers and employees alike get frustrated with the other when reasonable expectations go unmet. Management may call the declining enthusiasm "low employee engagement," describing it in a way that respects the privilege of power by putting the burden on workers to shape up and obey. If employees aren't as interested in their jobs anymore, management may believe it's their problem. When employee surveys designed to measure engagement or satisfaction yield disappointing results, positional power allows management the privilege of discounting unflattering feedback, leaving their original conclusions about employee behaviors and motivations intact.

Immediate supervisors play an outsized role in how employees feel about their employer according to Gallup research detailed in the book *It's the Manager.* Managers assign work, provide direction, evaluate performance, influence raises, champion promotions, and for all practical purposes *are* the employer. Yet, they rarely examine how they might be contributing to low employee satisfaction, engagement, or retention.

Left unresolved, mutual disappointment negatively impacts workplace relationships. When management fails to restore equilibrium to the $y+ = x+$ equation, the gap intensifies. The imbalance creates emotional overdraft charges, and when the cost gets too high, it leads to voluntary or involuntary separation.

The situation isn't much better when disappointed employees stay. The social contract merely reaches a new set point of $x = y$. No pluses. That's why when management gets the non-monetary portion of the employment relationship wrong it creates a downward spiral that takes employee satisfaction and engagement with it.

Whoa! Why is it management's responsibility to fix this employee problem? Why can't employees just step up? It sounds like we're supposed to do a bunch of handholding. You can't seriously expect me to be responsible for what someone else thinks is fair. All this feelings stuff . . . I'm not a therapist.

No one expects managers to be therapists. Yet how employees feel about whether management is keeping up their end of the implied social contract is within the scope of leadership responsibility.

Good asset stewardship, the responsible management of assets left in a supervisor's care, includes safeguarding the human capital assets represented by its labor force. Leadership is the ability to influence others to achieve common organizational goals. But if management's influence diminishes due to the low employee satisfaction or engagement that they've inspired, they have in essence wasted and reduced the value of an asset needed to move the business forward. That's irresponsible and *poor* asset stewardship. It's unfair to the organization whose assets are mismanaged and unfair to the employees whose well-being and ability to perform are mismanaged.

FAIRNESS FACTOR

Fairness is about good asset stewardship.

Wishing the problem away because management is in the driver's seat and can do what it wants is similar to overlooking a car's flashing engine light. Things break down when warnings are disregarded. Ignoring how management behavior affects employees operates similarly. Turning a blind eye when they know, or *should have known*, there is a management problem reflects negligence in exercising the duty of care needed to protect the organization's assets. Some might even go so far as to call it management malpractice.

Betraying the implied social contract, knowingly or unknowingly, has serious consequences, significantly impacting perceptions of organizational support and citizenship behavior according to research by Nichole Ballou at San Jose State University. Years of Gallup polls showing consistently low employee engagement levels tell a similar story.

Time for a reality check. Below is a summary of what the covenants of good faith and fair dealing in the implied employee-employer contract, and Maslow's Hierarchy of Human Motivational Needs teach us about the need for fairness at work:

- ✓ Fairness is about belonging.
- ✓ Fairness is about esteem.
- ✓ Fairness is about acting in good faith and with fair dealing.
- ✓ Fairness is about honest compensation and safe working conditions.
- ✓ Fairness is about providing employees with reasonable support, so they can do their jobs.
- ✓ Fairness is about good asset stewardship.

Employees are well aware of how economic power in the employee-employer relationship favors the employer and how it creates a strong desire to please those in authority who can influence their income and career advancement. Sadly, that imbalance of power also allows management to be less attentive to reasonable workforce expectations and gives rise to the unspoken norms nobody wants to talk about that crush employee satisfaction, engagement, and retention.

Chapter 2

The Norms Nobody
Wants to Talk About

Managers often want organizational culture to grow organically, expecting it to be nurtured by the company's vision and mission statements. Those missives often espouse aspirational values, such as dignity, respect, and obeying the law – standards no reasonable person would argue with. Similar to legal enabling statutes, they set boundaries for what's encouraged, discouraged, accepted, and rejected by the organization. But they're merely aspirational words.

When new employees ask how things work in a company, they're typically handed an employee handbook and an organization chart. That skeletal diagram of boxes and reporting relationships is a terrific resource of how authority and control is distributed. Each solid and dotted line is a micro-climate shaped by the support received from and the communication chemistry among those in the surrounding boxes. It's the *quality* of those connections that explains why an employee can have a terrific working relationship with one supervisor and a terrible experience with their replacement despite doing the same high caliber work in the same job.

Some people who have been employed in the workplace for a length of time learn that organizations tolerate certain habits and idiosyncrasies that deviate from its mission statement.

These behaviors may include excusing uncivil conduct from certain people in power or turning a blind eye to open secrets. They're often referred to as quirks, peccadillos, or double standards, with the people committing these deeds treated as sacred cows. Nonetheless, such acts

31

always represent a subjective ego, not rules, based set of customs associated with the benefit of power that define the true character and personality of the organization. It's those eccentricities that employees navigate every day and how things *really* work in the company. They're the norms nobody wants to talk about. Employees tolerate these norms with clenched teeth. That's why improving employee satisfaction, engagement, and retention requires a closer look at these workplace undertows.

Look, life isn't fair. That's just the way it is. Why does the workplace need to be fair when the rest of our existence isn't?

To get work done through others at work requires cooperation. Fairness greases those wheels by giving everyone something they want and need. Fairness is not about charity. It's smart business.

We are constantly evaluating whether someone is a friend or foe. The amygdala, the brain's built-in threat detector linked to our primal survival instinct, is constantly firing up and filtering messages in the presence of positional authority because *how* power is exercised determines whether employees' motivational needs (à la Maslow) are met or endangered. Employees are always watching to see how leaders put those vision and mission statements into practice, whether those principles are applied consistently, and whether managements' actions reflect good faith and fair dealing. Actions really do speak louder than words.

"Your actions speak so loudly I cannot hear what you are saying."
~Ralph Waldo Emerson

Everything executives, managers, and entrepreneurs say and do gets amplified whether they realize it or not. They're always "on" and endlessly being observed and scrutinized by workers for clues reflecting on the employees' own physical and emotional safety as well as financial well-being.

Why Unfairness Silently Kills Employee Engagement

When employees' expectations of good faith and fair dealing collide with the realities of workplace culture, the disconnect causes self-doubt about the reasonableness of their beliefs and expectations. This insecurity provides wiggle room for organizations to leverage their power of the purse and take advantage of the situation.

After employees process their initial shock about what they're experiencing, they start to conform. It creates their new normal because it's far easier and safer to go along and get along in order to stay employed.

Obeying and conforming sometimes happens unconsciously according to behavioral psychologists Solomon Asch and Stanley Milgram. That phenomenon might at first glance sound great to managers, but despite outward appearances, behavioral scientist Evan W. Carr finds that 40% of employees report feeling isolated and that those feelings of exclusion cause low employee engagement.

Carr's conclusions are hardly surprising. Just because employees put up with unfairness doesn't mean they've changed their core values, amended the implied social contract with their employer, or forgiven its breaches. They still want fairness. It's merely loss aversion that causes them to accept and obey the status quo to keep the pay and benefits coming.

If it's so unfair, why do employees stay?

Employees may accept trade-offs and stay in unsatisfying jobs for a variety of reasons. They might excuse it as paying their dues to work in their chosen field, the price of working for a high-powered organization or an influential individual, as a countdown to retirement or the vesting of certain benefits, and/or as supporting family with medical insurance in the face of a chronic illness. But the ultimate price of conforming is rarely a fixed cost. It's variable. And it's cumulative.

Perceptions of unfairness operate on a continuum. The degree to which employees start rebalancing the implied social contract, the $y+ = x+$ equation, depends on the severity, frequency, and duration of the offending behavior. But as the cost of continually burying their own needs and subordinating their better judgment to everyone else's rises, so too does the magnitude and degree of social contract violations; until one day they hit their limit. At that point it only takes a small injustice for them to say, *I can't take this anymore.*

That tipping point can land with a thud as it did for one head of environmental affairs at a manufacturing company who, without notice, decided to not return to work after her vacation. It could arrive with a fatal bang is it did for a company near Orlando, Florida, when a recently fired employee returned to the workplace and shot and killed 5 former co-workers.

Or it could land as a dramatic exit as a did in 2010 for a career JetBlue flight attendant who after 20 years of service had enough when a passenger retrieved their luggage too soon from the overhead bin, accidently hit the attendant on the head, and refused to apologize. Blasting the traveler over the plane's public address system while activating the aircraft's emergency evacuation slide, the attendant ended his tirade with "It's been great," grabbed a beer from the beverage cart, and jumped out.

Obedience and conformity are no substitutes for genuine fairness. Managers may turn a blind eye to fairness in the workplace, either by shrugging their shoulders and denying responsibility, saying there's nothing they can do about it, or excusing it altogether as a cost of doing business. These responses desensitize the organization, normalize the inequity, and embed unfairness into the company's culture.

Willful blindness to problematic behavior creates "dark corners" according to human resource guru and HR Culture Czar, Jim Jeffers. Employee engagement suffers and discretionary effort ceases to exist. It's where "fear replaces care," he says, creating "zombie employees coming to work and doing just what they have to do to get by."

Yet, creating an environment where employees are self-motivated is what drives the bottom line and organizations forward. That makes untangling the workplace norms that nobody seems to want to talk about a necessary first step in identifying employee engagement speed bumps.

FAIRNESS FACTOR

Fairness is about creating an environment that
reasonably supports self-motivation and discretionary effort.

Five Common Categories of Dispiriting Workplace Norms

Our work is personal. That's why to understand what depletes employee engagement it's instructive to look at management behaviors through the *employees'* lens of good faith and fair dealing and our basic human motivational needs. What follows is therefore an analysis of the five hot-button categories, or the common unwritten workplace norms nobody wants to talk about:

- unapproachability
- lack of recognition
- bias
- poor conflict management
- poor workload management

It's easy to dismiss the norms nobody wants to talk about when they're viewed in isolation one at a time, and to discount complainers as overly sensitive and whiny. But when we look at these norms in the aggregate, as in Figure 2.1 next page, it's easier to appreciate how they punch holes in our profound human need for good faith and fair dealing, and negatively impact employee engagement.

1. Unapproachability

Being unapproachable is off-putting and alienating. It affects employees' sense of belonging and esteem because physical and psychological distance, both real and imagined, makes it hard for employees to connect and get the information or help they need to successfully do their jobs. A heavy travel schedule, for example, a closed office door, and even power walking from point A to point B can send the message *I'm busy, not now.* But it begs the question, *When?*

How we communicate with each other can have a huge bearing on approachability. Is the tone dismissive or intimidating? Is the conversation abrupt or cut short? The impact can be especially acute for remote workers. Infrequent contact and terse exchanges, for example, can leave them feeling adrift and wondering whether they're being taken for granted.

	GOOD FAITH BASIC NEEDS		FAIR DEALING PSYCHOLOGICAL		OTHER INJUSTICE	
	Safety	Physiological	Esteem	Belonging	Legal Liability	Moral Injury
Unapproachability						
Unavailability			●	●		
Ignoring/Shunning			●	●		●
Lack of Empathy			●	●		●
Lack of Recognition						
Wage Theft		●	●	●	●	
Timely Compensation		●	●	●	●	
Subjective Rewards		●	●	●		●
Credit Stealing	●		●	●	●	●
No Feedback			●	●		
Bias						
Microaggressions	●		●	●		●
Bullying	●		●	●	●	●
Discrimination	●	●	●	●	●	●
Harassment	●	●	●	●	●	●
Poor Conflict Management						
Volatility	●	●	●	●		●
Conflict Avoidance			●	●	●	●
Gaslighting	●		●	●		●
Retaliation	●	●	●	●	●	●
Poor Workload Management						
Unclear Communications				●		
Micromanaging	●		●	●		●
Unrealistic Goals	●	●	●	●		●
Lack of Support	●	●	●	●		●

Figure 2.1 How the Most Common Workplace Norms Betray Fairness

It's even worse when managers allow themselves to be distracted and fail to give employees their full attention during a conversation. Such behavior conveys a lack of interest and empathy that can make workers feel ignored and "less than." It can even make them afraid to ask questions out of fear they'll be deemed incompetent.

Non-verbal behaviors can convey powerful messages. Making a U-turn in the hall because a manager forgot something could be an innocent move, but if the about face happens every time they see their least favorite employee it can feel like a slap in the face to that person. Shunning is a form of isolation. It negates a sense of belonging by making people invisible.

Oh please, these are such minor things. This stuff happens all the time. Management is incredibly busy.

Yes, that's true. It does happen every day. That's exactly the problem. It may be minor to management. But it's not trifling to employees when they don't have an opportunity to access the support needed to do their best work. Employees need to know when management has time for them. Unavailability runs counter to the covenant of fair dealing and the duty to not hinder an employee's performance under the implied employee-employer contract. Yet not being able to access necessary information or resources in a timely manner does exactly that.

FAIRNESS FACTOR

Fairness is about having reasonable access to management support.

It's one thing when management is occasionally unreachable. That's completely understandable. After all, we know they have responsibilities that go beyond sitting around and waiting for direct reports to ask questions.

But care must be taken regarding the magnitude, frequency, and duration of unavailability and to provide employees alternate means of accessing the support needed to carry on with their jobs. Being unreachable too often is demotivating. Research shows such absentee leadership is more isolating to employees than being treated poorly.

2. Lack of Recognition

Fair recognition is about being seen and given a voice. It's a motivational form of esteem and often thought of in terms of wages, raises, and promotions. A lack of recognition can also occur by playing favorites among employees or ignoring raised hands at meetings. It marginalizes an employee's sense of belonging, and as with unavailability, whether it happens and how often it happens factors into how damaging it is to the workplace relationship.

Lack of recognition can be seen in several areas:
- wages
- credit stealing

- no feedback
- bias
- microaggressions
- bullying

FAIRNESS FACTOR

Fairness is about being seen and heard.

a. Wages

When it comes to recognition, wages, raises, and promotions get the lion's share of attention because they affect our ability to earn a living so that we may meet our physiological necessities and our psychological need for esteem. The degree to which they represent honest compensation also influences our perceptions of whether our employer is acting in good faith. Multi-level marketing companies such as Mary Kay Inc. are prime examples of how recognition can be structured to incentivize self-motivating discretionary behavior.

FAIRNESS FACTOR

Fairness is about reasonably recognizing
and honoring the value of work.

Sometimes organizations engage in wage theft, the practice of not providing workers with honest compensation, whether by miscounting hours, by demanding off-the-clock services, or by mischaracterizing their status as salaried. Such practices are not only unfair, they're illegal. So is not paying workers in a timely fashion. Each jurisdiction has different labor law requirements making it incumbent on management to understand and follow them.

FAIRNESS FACTOR

Fairness is about following the rule of law.

The equal pay for equal work dilemma goes even further, taking recognition into a sensitive area of bias, particularly unlawful discrimination. Yet looking at the issue from purely a recognition perspective, the unwillingness to level the payroll playing field communicates through disparate compensation that one type of person, rather than the value of their work product, is *seen* as more worthy of more financial recognition. Such devaluation belies the notion of honest compensation and simultaneously attacks employees' ability to earn a living and esteem. That's why the failure to provide equal pay for equal work is fundamentally unfair.

Leaders can't reasonably expect blind loyalty from workers they openly see, and treat, as second-class citizens, especially when the same people who excuse unfair pay practices would be deeply upset if *their* work product were disrespected in the same way due to stereotypes beyond their control.

FAIRNESS FACTOR
Fairness is about equal pay for equal work.

b. Credit Stealing

While financial remuneration factors significantly into perceptions of good faith and fair dealing, recognition also refers to respecting employee strengths, giving them autonomy to use their strengths, and giving credit where credit is due. Taking employees for granted by ignoring the value of their contributions without a simple thank you is demotivating over time. Not only is the lack of this common courtesy impolite, it's disrespectful and violates the notion of fair dealing. After a while, such ungratefulness makes employees wonder whether what they do matters.

Yet, the most destructive way managers short-circuit recognition and the ability to connect with employees is by taking credit for their work and ideas. It's a top workplace relationship deal-breaker and morale-killer.

Part of the value of our ideas is the prestige it confers on us according to research conducted by Professors Joseph Henrich and Francisco J. Gil-White. When a boss takes credit for an employee's ideas without attribution, the boss essentially robs the employee of the idea's reputational value to confer more prestige on themselves. It's stealing. It's being dishonest, and it's a flagrant violation of the implied social contract.

Other research by psychologists Alex Shaw, Vivian Li, and Kristina Olson tells us that children as young as six years old care about their ideas and are deeply attached to them. What that means for us as adults in the workforce is that on an instinctive basis, we *know* taking someone else's work without giving proper credit is just plain *wrong*. It's unfair.

It's therefore no surprise that resentment builds when someone cheats an employee out of recognition for their work. It doesn't matter whether it's the boss who passes it off as their own and pockets the credit and financial reward, or the colleague who misappropriates an idea during a meeting and is praised while the person who said it first got ignored. Either way, the six-year-old inside shrieks in white-hot anger. The employee's ability and opportunity to engage with the organization and the autonomy to use their strengths has been usurped by an imposter. It's stressful. It's infuriating. It's wrong.

───────────(FAIRNESS FACTOR)───────────
Fairness is about giving credit where due
and not stealing someone else's ideas or work product.

Wielding power for personal gain to burnish a reputation at someone else's expense sets up a win-lose dynamic. Collaboration and sense of belonging, as well as psychological safety, take a backseat when employees are afraid of being cheated. If an employee has legal rights in their work product, stealing credit can also lead to lawsuits.

c. No Feedback

Poor feedback is another common way employees experience a lack of recognition in the workplace, and it was brought to mind during a routine dental visit when my hygienist asked what I was working on. I told her about this book, and she immediately said, "I know what you mean."

"How so?" I asked.

When she first joined the dental practice, she had an idea to improve office operations. As part of the team, she thought her observations would be welcome. But they didn't implement or discuss them with her in any way. Zip. Nada. Crickets.

A month or so later, she made another suggestion. Again, the silence was deafening. After her third idea went nowhere, she stopped offering suggestions. "Why bother?" she said.

Getting ignored once could be excused as the person being too busy at the time. It happens. Move on. The second time it occurred a few weeks later, she was more on the fence, wondering "What's going on?" After three strikes she reluctantly got the message.

It's no surprise the hygienist stepped back. Her silence became a way to reclaim her power. It was a form of withdrawal, of employee blowback, an example of diminishing employee engagement. Thankfully, she still put the sparkle back in my smile, but any thoughts of taking initiative or doing more for her employer went down the drain.

"Speaking up isn't worth it," she said.

What an interesting choice of words. It wasn't *worth it*. There was no value in speaking up, no recognition. The hygienist was ignored as a person. She wasn't part of the conversation.

FAIRNESS FACTOR

Fairness is about recognizing employees' good intentions.

What kind of *value* could she have reasonably expected? What could have reasonably preserved or nurtured her discretionary efforts? Some acknowledgement would have been a good start.

"Thanks for bringing that idea to our attention. We do it this way because of x, y, z," said in a helpful tone would have let her know she had been seen and heard and would also have created a teachable moment that generated goodwill. Providing context would have brought her inside the circle of how and why things were being done the way they were.

Who knows, she might have built upon that with an even better idea. They'll never know. Nonetheless, a little gratitude would have signaled appreciation to the hygienist as a person who was merely trying to help. It would have gone a long way to keep her engaged. Instead, the organization's inaction communicated that she didn't deserve an answer. It basically said, "We don't care what you think. Mind your own business." It made her invisible.

No one likes being ignored. Absolutely. No. One. Recognition matters. (Come to think of it, she was no longer working there at my last visit.)

It's easy to think of recognition only in monetary terms: bonuses, prizes, raises, and promotions. Occasionally, thank-you notes and "job well done" get added to the mix. But it's no substitute for day-to-day respect, something that bias can destroy.

d. Bias

Bias drives a stake into the heart of fairness and employee engagement because it drowns out facts with preconceived notions that can either favor or prejudice individuals due to factors beyond their immediate control. Bias is basically a form tribalism. How it impacts our sense of belonging and esteem in an organization depends on whether we're part of the in-crowd.

When bias reveals favoritism, it promotes privilege and elevates the sense of self, contributing to perceptions of superiority. When bias exposes intolerance, it disadvantages employees by attacking their esteem, potentially threatening their physical safety and ability to earn a living with behaviors ranging from microaggressions to bullying, outright discrimination, and/or harassment. Research by Princeton psychology professor Susan Fiske, for example, finds that bias is closely related to the ability to control resources in organizations. It's about power.

In working with organizations around the world, neuroscience educator Sarah Peyton echoed Fiske's findings and made a fascinating discovery of her own about power differentials between majorities and minorities in the workplace. The more we're different from 70% of the predominant workforce composition, the more we lose our foothold in the organization's power structure she told me during our

Business Confidential Now interview. For example, if 70% of employees are white males and you're a white male, you already have an easier time fitting in and connecting. If you're not a white male, it's harder. How much harder? How much bias will you encounter? It depends.

What's critical about Peyton's finding is how it highlights the importance of *acceptance and inclusion* by co-workers as central to employees' sense of belonging. That makes the criteria for inclusion or exclusion the subject of deep interest and concern for employees. They want to know whether their status is based on merit or unfair stereotypes.

───── (**FAIRNESS FACTOR**) ─────
Fairness is about legitimate acceptance and inclusion.

Acceptance and inclusion don't happen by osmosis. If employees are not being intentionally included, they risk being *un*intentionally excluded because obeying and conforming can mask implicit, unconscious, or systemic barriers such as glass ceilings that dampen full employee participation.

In the 1980s, for example, when more women were flocking into the workplace the notion of diversity was often nothing more than tokenism and fitting in was what I call "Randy in a Skirt." In other words, the male power structure wasn't terribly welcoming of a minority's point of view. They really didn't want to hear it. The prevailing sentiment conveyed through subtle and not so subtle signals and cues was that women should be seen and not heard. Organizations wanted the appearance of diversity, and if women insisted on having a voice, it was in their best interest to parrot the party line and not be disruptive. Voilà! "Randy in a Skirt." Conform and obey.

Minorities of all stripes initially faced similar resistance and genuine lack of belonging because they often had to suppress or minimize their voice, appearance, and even values, so as not to offend the sensibilities of an organization's dominant white male power structure. Sadly, many minorities *still* fear bringing their authentic self to the workplace because they want to minimize being the target of microaggressions, bullying, discrimination, or harassment. Unfortunately, the benefit of diversity is lost without an inclusive culture to support it.

FAIRNESS FACTOR

Fairness is about treating the least favorite employee
the same as the favorite.

e. Microaggressions

Microaggressions are subtle slights that inappropriately single employees out based on their race, gender, ethnic origin, or sexual orientation. It includes behaviors such as patting a pregnant employee's tummy or touching African American hair without permission, mistaking male nurses for doctors and female doctors for nurses, challenging a person of color standing in the priority boarding lane at the airport, the male supervisor telling a female employee their report *wasn't bad for a girl*, or regularly snubbing a gay colleague from drinks after work with co-workers.

FAIRNESS FACTOR

Fairness is about maintaining decorum.

Assumptions based on stereotypes are hurtful because they challenge identity and sense of belonging in a negative way. It doesn't matter whether the offending behavior is accidental, intentional, or done in jest. For example, when an executive kept mispronouncing his assistant's name despite continued efforts to correct him, he started to do it on purpose thinking it was humorous. She quit.

It reminds me of a friend who worked for one of the big three Detroit car makers for 17 years. "In the beginning senior management knew your name," he said. "Then things changed, and you became a number." It diminished his sense of belonging, and he ultimately left to open a bicycle shop in Maine. Boom.

Are names a big deal to employees? Absolutely. Ignoring a name is a form of shunning. Turning a name into a number is dehumanizing. And mispronouncing it on purpose is dismissive and insulting.

(**FAIRNESS FACTOR**)

Fairness is about respecting the employee by respecting their name.

f. Bullying

Bullying is even worse. It happens when people in positions of power intentionally and repeatedly harm, intimidate, or coerce someone they perceive as vulnerable. A 2021 survey done by the Workplace Bullying Institute of American adults found 30% suffered abusive conduct at work, another 19% witness it, a total of 49% were affected by it, and 66% were aware that it happens. Sadly, the research also found that remote workers suffered more bullying than their in-office counter parts, with 50% experiencing it in meetings and 9% via email.

Even more disheartening, employer reactions measured by the same survey revealed 60% of management attitudes and behaviors actually enabled bullying: 13% encouraged it believing it's necessary for a competitive organization, 11% defended it when the bullies were one of their own (i.e. managers), 11% rationalized it saying it's routine, 16% denied it happens and failed to investigate complaints, and 9% discounted it claiming it's not harmful. It's no wonder bullying is an entrenched workplace norm that nobody wants to talk about.

Unfortunately bullying in all of its incarnations *is* harmful. It's a form of manipulation that causes stress and stress-related diseases and is a form of psychological harm because it isolates people. It can also escalate into physical and cyber assaults and is illegal in some countries. Of course, whether it rises to the level of serious legal exposure is highly dependent on the facts of each case and should be discussed with local counsel.

(**FAIRNESS FACTOR**)

Fairness is about being reasonably tolerant,
not badgering or menacing.

In the United States, for example, bullying can cross the line into illegal discrimination when the coercion and intimidation are due to an employee's status in what's known as a protected class. It's when cruelty is inflicted due to the employee's age, race, color, sex, religion, or national origin. And depending on the nature of the duress, it could also be viewed as illegal harassment, including *quid pro quo* sexual harassment when job offers, promotions and raises, for example, are dependent on sexual favors.

3. Poor Conflict Management

Bullying is often a result of poor conflict management. When expectations go unmet and bad news is delivered or disappointing performance is observed, it's easy for our amygdala to interpret it as a threat and highjack the decision-making process. A leader's emotional volatility and inability to self-regulate can send people diving for cover in fear. It's extremely difficult to feel secure or have a sense of belonging when a manager is shouting, screaming, cursing, or humiliating employees in front of others. It makes workers reluctant to raise problems or deliver bad news for fear of being automatically blamed or losing their jobs. Playing a blame game is not constructive problem solving, nor is retaliating against the employee who brings legitimate concerns to management's attention.

FAIRNESS FACTOR

Fairness is about not jumping to conclusions before the facts are known.

What's worse is when management pretends there is no problem, gaslighting employees by challenging their perception of reality and claiming they're overreacting, too sensitive, or taking things too personally. But ignoring problems or shifting responsibility doesn't solve anything. It's merely another way managers silently destroy employee engagement.

When a head of consumer focus groups, for example, continued to receive hostile phone calls and unreasonable demands from an irate client about scheduling and test results, he asked his supervisor to kindly intercede with a phone call. The bullying from the client was so awful he threatened to quit if management failed to make the call. Unfortunately, his boss let him fend for himself and the lack support left him feeling isolated. "You can only put up with being yelled at by a client for so long," he said. And as soon as he gave notice "a huge weight lifted off [his] shoulders."

FAIRNESS FACTOR
Fairness is about protecting employees
from unreasonable workplace threats.

4. Poor Workload Management

Poor workload management is another way organizations fall short of meeting their duty of fair dealing and providing reasonable support by not interfering or failing to cooperate in an employee's job performance.

Unfortunately, lack of support is sometimes viewed through the narrow lens of not offering enough rah-rah encouragement or appreciation for a job well done. It then gets shrugged off as warm and fuzzy coddling real adults shouldn't need and management doesn't have time for. However, inadequate staffing or raw materials and not making accurate information available in a timely fashion also qualify as lack of meaningful management support, as do insufficient training and unclear communications, such as vague or incomplete instructions.

FAIRNESS FACTOR
Fairness is about giving employees reasonable
support to do their jobs successfully.

Micromanaging also fits the bill since it directly interferes with someone trying to do their work by constantly looking over their shoulder and second-guessing their decisions.

FAIRNESS FACTOR
Fairness is about respecting employees' skills and need for autonomy.

Even certain goals can signify a lack of support when they represent wishful thinking more than attainable reality. Unrealistic goals can be one of the most insidious ways leaders undermine employee engagement. After all, nobody likes to fail, and we hate being set up to fail by things beyond our control even more. It's the very essence of unfairness.

Fairness is about not setting employees up to fail.

Please don't misunderstand. Stretch goals can be a good thing. They're aspirational, and there is nothing wrong with that. But even aspirational goals need periodic reality checks, otherwise they make management look out of touch and incompetent.

Take for example a large electronics manufacturer where a friend worked that set an annual 10% cost-cutting goal for each component sourced through their purchasing department. In the early days of a new product's commercialization, when production volumes steadily increase, competitive bidding among qualified vendors and volume discounts make hitting the 10% target highly realistic, attainable, and desirable. Economies of scale can and should be leveraged in the early stages of commercialization to negotiate more favorable pricing as higher volumes lower individual unit costs.

But volumes eventually plateau and taper off when product cycles mature and get eclipsed by newer 2.0 versions. At some point with vendor profit margins squeezed razor thin by prior large volume purchases it is unrealistic to expect additional 10%-unit cost reductions year after year as volumes *decrease*. At some point vendors would be selling components at a loss. They'd be irresponsible to do so.

Yet raises and bonuses of employees in the purchasing department, who were specialized and organized by product line, were contingent on continuously achieving additional 10% cost savings every year no matter what. Over time it meant they were penalized for product cycle maturities that were inevitable and beyond their control. Many sought transfers or left the company when blamed for not achieving what had now become impossible.

Customer service employees at a medical billing firm experienced a similar lack of management support. Believe it or not, they were only given 30 seconds per call to do their job. Calls were tracked. If more than 30 seconds was spent on a call, a formula converted a percentage of the overage into a dollar amount that was deducted from the employee's annual bonus.

When was the last time anyone called a customer service number at a company and got a complete and satisfactory answer in under 30 seconds? Callers were probably on hold for what seemed like forever and told by a closed loop audio recording to check the company's website (which they did and found useless), and then directed to an "instant" chat (which was slow and "manned" by a dumb robot). Even when they finally reached a real person instead of artificial intelligence, answered the security questions to verify their identity and account, and remembered why they called, their 30 seconds expired yesterday.

What kind of service can someone provide if they're primary goal is to end the call as quickly as possible instead of listening to understand the problem and continuing to help until the issue is fully resolved? Where is the *customer* in customer service? Imagine what that does to those who take genuine pride in helping people solve problems and who deeply care about the customer experience. Imagine how incredibly frustrating and demoralizing that is.

Needless to say, the best customer service employees left the medical billing firm. Their sense of accomplishment in a job well done, of meaning in their work, of belonging, and trust in management support was utterly destroyed by a metric detached from reality.

"Sometimes you just stop banging your head against the wall," one executive vice president told me. "The wall is still there. But by not banging your head against it you feel better." In other words, you stop trying your hardest. You back down, obey, and conform. Or you leave.

Moral Injury

The last column of Figure 2.1, moral injury, deserves special attention. It refers to the acute emotional distress certain workplace norms can inflict. Unlike burnout that focuses on an individual's inability to cope with chronic stress, moral injury concentrates on the system and culture where an employee is in a high-stakes situation and is being asked or required to betray what's morally right by someone with legitimate authority over them. Another way to think of it is as harm resulting from a deep ethical conflict of interest, one that challenges our sense of right and wrong, our deepest values, and what we stand for.

Moral injury is not a new concept and is most often associated with the military and the psychological distress soldiers experience being unprepared for the intense emotional consequences of their role in times of war. For many, those experiences lead to post-traumatic stress disorder.

Moral injury can also occur in occupations outside of the armed forces. It can result from an acute trauma, such as high-stakes business decisions requiring unacceptable moral compromises, such as cooking the books to satisfy a huge merger or misrepresenting data to obtain regulatory approval of a new drug.

It can also result from a prolonged series of lesser traumas, a psychological death-by-a-thousand-cuts scenario, where prolonged exposure to bullying, harassment, systemic discrimination, and/or microaggressions that are often invisible to everyone else provokes fear and deeply affects an employee's sense of safety and self.

In one such fear-based culture, the constant beatdown caused one person to confide in me, "I wish I was a ditch digger because at least I'd be able to raise my head once in a while." Other employees coped with the chronic incivility by quiet quitting, prescription anti-depressants, alcohol, and other means. It was heartbreaking to hear and see. Of those who moved on, many said it took several years to feel like themselves again. That's how crushing moral injury can be to mental health.

(**FAIRNESS FACTOR**)

Fairness is about preserving the spirit of the implied
social contract by caring about employees' mental health.

Moral injury can also result from the inherent dangers of the job. During the COVID-19 pandemic, for example, nurses, doctors, first responders, and other health-care workers witnessed hospital wards overflowing with patients facing life-threatening conditions we knew little about at the time. They worked punishing overtime hours, often without sufficient personal protective equipment. In addition to risking their own lives and potentially their families', they confronted agonizing decisions about how to prioritize scarce resources to ease their patients' suffering. The toll on these workers led to physical and emotional exhaustion and moral injury causing many of them to leave not just their jobs but their profession. According to a McKinsey study it's a phenomenon contributing to severe staffing shortages that strain the operations of health-care providers to meet patient needs.

The plight of U.S. long-haul truckers offers another sad example. Deregulation in the 1980s aimed at reducing transportation costs to consumers led to driver wage cuts, allowing trucking companies to pay drivers by the mile and exclude the substantial wait times during on loading or off-loading periods. It basically meant drivers could be on the job and not get paid. To compensate, they'd make up for lost time on the road by speeding and creating safety hazards for motorists.

Subsequent regulations requiring monitoring devices to track break times and the number of hours on the road appeared to remedy that problem. But when the devices had no mechanism to take weather and rush hour road conditions into account, or more importantly the driver's own assessment of whether they feel well enough or awake enough to drive, they only served to compound existing safety threats. As a result of these working conditions, the industry averages an annual driver turnover of 100%, with some overachieving companies experiencing a 300% rate.

The lack of social support for the drivers as evidenced by a system that incentivizes speeding to make up for unpaid wait times, puts drivers and other motorists at physical risk of colliding with an 80,000-pound semi traveling at 75 miles an hour. This system also requires drivers to operate under any conditions, even when feeling unwell or too tired, forcing them to make ethical decisions about their personal safety and/ or ability to earn a living. Demanding that tradeoff is a deep betrayal of the covenants of good faith and fair dealing.

FAIRNESS FACTOR

Fairness is about mitigating dangers that can cause moral injury.

Employees living paycheck-to-paycheck doing inflexible, low-wage jobs whose shift hours are subject to change from week to week with little notice face a similar high-stakes dilemma. While their hourly rate could very well meet legal requirements, the inconsistent number of hours they receive generates unpredictable cash flow, making it hard to consistently pay rent, keep food on the table, or buy life-saving medicine. It can even lead to agonizing choices between paying utilities and buying groceries or accessing healthcare. It's basically not a living wage that reasonably satisfies Maslow's foundational physiological needs. Plus, the undependable work schedule turns arranging doctor's appointments and childcare into a nightmare, putting family safety and health at risk.

Finding a second job sounds like a reasonable way to close the financial gap, but erratic scheduling turns it into a nonviable option, leaving such employees constantly teetering on a financial knife edge, forcing them to choose among basic necessities. It's another example of how certain policies can inflict moral injury on employees.

FAIRNESS FACTOR

Fairness is about anticipating the consequences
of management decisions on all stakeholders.

While the damage imposed by moral injury is one of degree and operates on a continuum, affecting some people more than others. The psychological trauma and impact on mental health is very real for the person experiencing it. Research by King's College London finds morally injured people are at risk for developing mental health disorders, including depression.

In his book, *Dying for a Paycheck*, Jeffrey Pfeffer, Professor of Organizational Behavior at the Graduate School of Business at Stanford University, details research showing how harmful management practices are as detrimental to health, including mortality and being diagnosed with illness by a physician, as exposure to secondhand smoke.

Common sense tells us it is exceedingly difficult for employees to have the company's back when they can't trust the company to have theirs. Actually, it's impossible. Compromising the safety and physiological needs of employees and risking moral injury is therefore never a smart move if the goal is high employee engagement or retention. Yet, the problem persists.

If the impact of the norms nobody wants to talk about, as illustrated in Figure 2.1, look like a cluster bomb hit employee morale, it's because it has. The use of power is what enables the unproductive norms. Yet, we're reluctant to talk about power or scrutinize it. Our deference to it and fear of retaliation make it taboo to question or challenge it. But given its role in the norms nobody wants to talk about, our quest for fairness at work leaves us little choice. Our discussion would be spectacularly incomplete if its role were ignored. The more we understand power, the more we can use it responsibly to advance the mission of the organization, and improve employee satisfaction, engagement, and retention.

Time for another reality check. Below is a review of how the norms nobody wants to talk about impact the covenants of good faith and fair dealing of implied employee-employer contract and Maslow's Hierarchy of Human Motivational Needs and what they teach us about the need for fairness at work:

✓ Fairness is about creating an environment that reasonably support self-motivation and discretionary effort.

✓ Fairness is about having reasonable access to management support.

✓ Fairness is about being seen and heard.

✓ Fairness is about reasonably recognizing and honoring the value of work

✓ Fairness is about following the law.

✓ Fairness is about equal pay for equal work.

✓ Fairness is about giving credit where due and not stealing someone else's ideas or work product.

✓ Fairness is about recognizing employees' good intentions.

✓ Fairness is about legitimate acceptance and inclusion.

✓ Fairness is about treating the least favorite employee the same as the favorite.

✓ Fairness is about maintaining decorum.

✓ Fairness is about respecting the employee and respecting their name.

✓ Fairness is about being reasonably tolerant, not badgering or menacing.

✓ Fairness is about not jumping to conclusions before the facts are known.

✓ Fairness is about protecting employees from unreasonable workplace threats.

✓ Fairness is about giving employees reasonable support to do their jobs successfully.

✓ Fairness is about respecting employees' skills and need for autonomy.

✓ Fairness is about not setting employees up to fail.

✓ Fairness is about preserving the spirit of the implied social contract by caring about employees' mental health.

✓ Fairness is about mitigating dangers that can cause moral injury.

✓ Fairness is about anticipating the consequences of management decisions on all stakeholders.

Chapter 3

How Power Changes Everything

Power plays a pivotal role in the deployment of human capital, and efforts to talk about it are often stifled because speaking truth to power about power makes management extremely uncomfortable. It's a sensitive subject.

It's "much easier to talk about sex than it is to talk about power," wrote Harvard Business School Professor Rosabeth Moss Kanter in 1979. "People who have it deny it; people who want it do not appear to hunger for it; and people who engage in its machinations do so secretly." (From "*Power Failure in Management Circuits*" by Rosabeth Moss Kanter. Harvard Business Review, July 1979.)

Ironically, her words are as true today as they were decades ago. Nothing much has changed when it comes to how power is perceived and silently amassed in organizations. Research by professors Julie Battilana and Tiziana Casciaro, authors of *Power, for All*, build on Kanter's observations, finding that our perceptions of power are dogged by three harmful fallacies:

(1) the belief that power, once acquired, can be permanently owned;

(2) the assumption that power is purely positional, exclusive to those with rank and formal authority; and

(3) the notion that power is inherently dirty, acquired only through untoward means.

Power is neither inherently good nor evil. It's simply the ability to affect change. The more powerful someone is, the more they can achieve. But we all only have 24 hours in a day, and can't be experts on everything. We expand our influence and reach by successfully engaging and working through others.

The predicament management finds itself in with regard to low employee engagement supports Battilana and Casciaro's point that power cannot be permanently owned. After all, employees are never more engaged than on their first day at a new job. It's only after the new hires discover the norms nobody wants to talk about that their enthusiasm drops faster than a new car depreciates when leaving a dealership. Management's positional power hasn't changed during that window of time, but its influence has due to the norms they enable and condone.

Indeed, the very phrase *low employee engagement* frames the dilemma in a way that respects the privilege of power by putting the burden on employees to shape up and obey. It reminds me of the bumper sticker: "The beatings will continue until morale improves." The focus is always on fixing employees because deference to power automatically gives leaders the positional benefit of the doubt. One vice president, for example, told me she knew she had "made it" when she discovered senior management would take her word over her direct reports'.

The unfortunate consequences of embracing this common power paradigm are two-fold: (a) it separates the workforce into "us-versus-them" groups that lionizes the powerful, and (b) it discourages honest communication by those with less power because their desire for belonging and job security promotes conformance. How power is recognized, appreciated, and exercised is pivotal to whether the promise of high employee engagement in the implied social contract between employees and employers is realized and why a deeper understanding of power is critical to demystifying unfairness at work.

FAIRNESS FACTOR

Fairness is about appreciating the pivotal role of power in
the implied social contract between employees and employers.

Wait a minute! Are you suggesting managers should give up their power to make things equal? Why would I want to do that? There's status and privilege associated with my positional power. I worked hard to get where I am!

I respect the sacrifices individuals make to climb the corporate ladder or launch a business. New managers, whose careers up until their promotion have been focused solely on managing up the chain of command, discover they now have a new constituency: the people who report to them. Despite a leader's good intentions managing direct reports successfully requires different competencies than scrambling up the organizational chart or posting an "open for business" sign. Leadership and empowering employees are not a zero-sum game. They both call for soft skills, also known as emotional intelligence, to supplement and complement existing industry and business expertise.

The ability to honestly connect with people expands, rather than diminishes, a manager's sphere of influence and overall power. Best of all, authority stemming from robust workplace relationships grounded in mutual respect and healthy boundaries is more enduring than positional, command-and-control power plays. Such authority engenders more employee trust and loyalty because it reflects more good faith and fair dealing.

FAIRNESS FACTOR

Fairness is about exercising power consistent with
the principles of good faith and fair dealing.

Power differentials are a fact of life in the workplace, but whether they contribute to the norms nobody wants to talk about depends on how well leaders can navigate the perils of power.

Power Changes What Employees Hear

People in authority are often unaware of how their position impacts what employees hear and take away from a conversation and how easily undue meaning is ascribed to even seemingly innocent comments. A supervisor might, for example, note the kindness of someone who brought donuts to share with co-workers and suddenly discover the calorie bombs appearing with increasing frequency. Even though the intent was to appreciate an employee's generosity, not a signal of how to curry favor, it's easy for intentions to get misconstrued when spoken by someone higher up.

Connecting with the audience is the responsibility of the speaker, not the listener, according to Alan Alda. He's famous for being the multi-talented, Emmy Award-winning actor best known for his role in the classic TV series M*A*S*H. What many might not know about him is his passionate dedication to the art and science of relating and communicating. He helped found the Center for Communicating Science at Stony Brook University in New York, where his primary mission is to help scientists explain their work in a way the public can easily grasp and understand.

In his book, *If I Understood You, Would I Have This Look on My Face?*, Alda insightfully notes how real communication happens when the listener "gets it," not merely hears it. Making sure our message is truly heard means watching and interpreting our audience's reactions. It requires both empathy and awareness.

Oh please, how am I supposed to do all that? When I'm talking, isn't it the employee's job to pay attention TO ME, their supervisor?

Yes, and they definitely do!

Employees are constantly watching and listening to what managers say and do as if their future and cash flow life depends on it. Because it does. Management *has* their attention. But is it the right kind of attention?

Consider whether what workers see and hear reflects good faith and fair dealing. Does it support inclusiveness, or encourage collaboration? Is it self-motivating? Or does it tie them into emotional knots and discourage them?

For management communications to stick the landing in a positive way leaders need to honestly connect with employees both procedurally and emotionally, as illustrated in Figure 3.1 on the next page. It's about paying attention to the context and subtext of their verbal and non-verbal messages because connecting, as Alda astutely observed, requires both awareness and empathy.

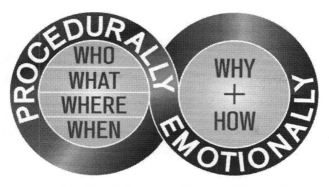

Figure 3.1 – How We Relate to and Connect with Each Other

FAIRNESS FACTOR

Fairness is about awareness and empathy.

Procedurally, the context of a message is about who the audience is, *what* we're trying to convey, *when* we convey it, and *where* we convey it. Those factors set the stage for our objective understanding of what's going on. On the emotional level where fairness lives, *why* and especially *how* these messages are conveyed provide subtext and nuance that influences our perceptions of good faith and fair dealing.

The following is a common example of these communication power dynamics at work.

The Case of the Office Meeting

In working with clients, I've discovered office meeting management provides fertile ground for power plays and communication hiccups. For the sake of this discussion, let's assume a manager invites the right people (the who); has a meaningful agenda (the what and the why); establishes the place, either in person or virtually (the where); but schedules the meeting to begin shortly before quitting time and gives the team very little notice (the when).

Management certainly has the positional authority to set the meeting for whenever it wants. Yet, the emotional tone of the message, asking people to stay late with little notice, displays a lack of empathy and respect for work/life boundaries and preexisting obligations, plus a lack of social awareness of how the last-minute request would be received by the team.

Sure, dutiful staff will attend the meeting and participate as good team players do, especially if they hold senior positions. But unless there is a true emergency requiring immediate attention (the why), it's unlikely problem-solving will be terribly robust. In the back of their mind employees will be thinking about what they're missing out on and will no doubt prefer to wrap up the meeting as soon as possible. High employee engagement is unlikely.

It's one thing if these hiccups happen occasionally. But, when they're frequent, or are due to management's persistent procrastination, it's an example of poor workload management, a norm nobody wants to talk about, and it takes a toll on staff.

Poor timing (the when) is but one example that can prompt a degree of employee blowback. Inviting the wrong people (who) to a meeting is another. Leave someone out whose role is necessary to implement what's being discussed and the lack of recognition dents their sense of belonging and safety. (*Is my job still secure?*)

When the same voices monopolize a meeting and no one else gets heard, the inability to be seen and to participate is frustrating. (*Do I matter?*) An unclear meeting agenda (what) makes employees wonder why their time is being wasted. Would a written summary (the how) accomplish the same thing instead of requiring attendance to hear others drone on? The same goes for meeting chairs who exercise poor time management by allowing attendees enamored of their voices to hijack the discussion with issues unrelated to the agenda. They all add up to poor workload management.

None of these common gaffes promote collaboration or a sense of belonging because they're tone deaf to employees' reasonable needs and/or fears. While management's positional authority certainly *permits* such use of power, the better question to ask is not *whether leaders can do it*, but rather *whether they should.*

> **FAIRNESS FACTOR**
> Fairness is about kindness and being considerate
> of employees needs and fears.

Leaders are wise to remember that workers subjecting themselves to someone more powerful in the workplace is a calculated risk, a potential danger, that's constantly being gauged. Employees need to know whether they can trust management, are safe, or in peril of losing a plum assignment, a raise, a promotion, or even their jobs.

The amygdala, our built-in threat filter, is a million times faster than our conscious mind according to Jill Ratliff, author of *Leadership Through Trust and Collaboration*. That's why *how* we communicate matters if we truly care about improving employee engagement and why the onus is on management to lead the way.

> **FAIRNESS FACTOR**
> Fairness is about respecting the employees' point of view.

Power Changes Management Too

Leaders may not realize how power changes people, including themselves. I'm not referring to the material aspects of higher pay, benefits, or status; or the oft-cited adage of how "power corrupts." Even when someone has the best of intentions, power can literally go to their head. Research by psychologists Briñol, Petty, Valle, Rucker, and Becerra reveals how power translates into confidence that magnifies and amplifies the thoughts of the more powerful, confirming their belief in being more right than anyone else. We've probably all experienced that phenomenon in the form of someone believing they're the "smartest one in the room." Sometimes they really are. Sometimes they're not.

Such confidence contributes to narratives of exceptionalism says Professor Dacher Keltner, author of the *Power Paradox*, giving managers permission to collaborate less with others. Power also makes people less inhibited according to research by Yale professor Michael W. Kraus. It activates their drive, energy, and emotion, giving them the freedom to express themselves in ways that are less attuned to how their behavior impacts or hurts others.

These dynamics can hinder employee engagement. It tosses aside the virtuous behavior that helped management gain influence in the first place and promotes an "us-versus-them" mindset that subsequently destroy the very relationships needed to maintain and expand management's power.

Using power to create a caste system tears at the foundation of teamwork. It's polarizing. There is a saying in the theater that there are no small roles, only small actors. If an employee didn't fill a meaningful role in an organization, however minor, employers wouldn't need them. That's why leaders wanting to inspire belonging and more employee engagement need to remember that everyone on the team matters. They each play an important part. You're in this together.

FAIRNESS FACTOR

Fairness is about remembering we're on the same team.

When it comes to fostering unity, power's unbridled freedom of expression is particularly troublesome. An "anything goes" spirit contributes to incivility and disrespect that trickles down into the workplace norms nobody wants to talk about by revealing internal values and biases that betray good faith and fair dealing. It represents an empathy deficit that can also send moral compasses spinning out of control when management reduces everything to numbers and focuses exclusively on the bottom line.

Workplace enablers who condone such corrosive conduct in the name of authenticity, saying "that's just the way so-and-so is," normalize the polarizing behavior and embed it into the workplace culture. It's a tactic typically used to preserve selfishness, and the right to say whatever someone wants regardless of whether it insults, offends, or intimidates anyone and, more importantly, to say it with zero accountability.

When it's allowed to happen without consequence, these excuses become entitlements that eclipse every other value in the company's mission statement. It's a wildly misdirected tactic if the goal is to increase employee engagement, and that's why it's necessary to expose the political correctness, wokeness, and free speech excuses used to defend and rationalize such disrespectful behavior as the ineffective fig leaves they are.

Fairness is about exercising power respectfully.

Debunking the Political Correctness and Wokeness Excuses

Words matter. I appreciate how easy it is to get defensive when someone challenges our self-awareness of what employees see and hear. Most of us think we're already communicating well.

We're in our own head about why we do certain things. Our words and actions are our friends. We love our friends. We don't want to believe they could be hurting anyone because we mean well. Besides, it's our truth, and no one wants to be censored.

Take the controversy over "Merry Christmas" versus "Happy Holidays." The political correctness police would have us believe one phrase is better than the other. Say the wrong thing and we're horrible people. The internal state of annoyance and anger such accusations produce lowers our ability to build trust regardless of where we stand in the debate. When it comes to attacking political correctness or being woke, each side views the other as being unreasonable and possibly even as "the enemy." Add to that our firm belief that we're "right," doubling down instead of backing down, and the situation gets worse. As a result, using political correctness or wokeness as an excuse to say whatever we want creates a no-win scenario that only drives us further apart.

Please, let's stop for a moment to set the emotional baggage down and clear the air.

The definition of political correctness is really nothing more than the *avoidance of expressions or actions that insult, exclude, or disadvantage people who are already experiencing social difficulty or discrimination.* Has the phrase been misused? Sure. But the objective is to do no harm, to not make things worse by compounding someone's existing social burden or minimizing their lived experiences by making them an object of disrespect.

The essence of political correctness dovetails with our need for inclusion and belonging, our shared humanity. Unfortunately, it's often used as a power play to exclude and demonize others.

Similarly, wokeness is a phrase that's heavily misused and politicized. It's about awareness plain and simple, and more specifically about awareness of racism and inequality. It's similar to political correctness in that it comes from a place of empathy and *tolerance* for people who are not like us. The goal is to promote respect and sidestep conflicts based on stereotypes and other false assumptions that contribute to bias. The unifying concept is empathy for our shared humanity.

Some people blur the concept of empathy with sympathy. But they're different in a very important way. Empathy is about seeing the world through someone else's eyes, about reading their emotions, or about walking a mile in their shoes as the Elvis Presley song says. It's about being open-minded. Sympathy, on the other hand, is viewing their situation only through our own lens.

FAIRNESS FACTOR

Fairness is about being open-minded.

I appreciate how "Happy Holidays" sounds more inclusive than "Merry Christmas," which only refers to the Christian tradition. Being more encompassing conveys a sense of belonging and kinship in the joy for these special celebrations regardless of how someone personally observes them.

Yet, if you know your audience is Christian, they may prefer "Merry Christmas" the same way someone who is Jewish would prefer "Happy Hanukkah," and so forth. Isn't it kinder? More thoughtful? And a touch more respectful because you're acknowledging and respecting that person's faith?

Of course, "Happy Holidays" is an easy default. But one-size-fits-all solutions are rarely as satisfying as customized ones. If you've ever tried on a one-size-fits-all shirt you know they're functional but not necessarily flattering. Tailoring improves fit the same way awareness and thoughtfulness improves relationships. If we're tone-deaf and get it wrong, we can appear out of touch or incompetent. Little things can mean a lot and tarnish our reputation even if we think we're only exercising our right to free speech.

Debunking the Free Speech Excuse

Oh yeah, so what about free speech?

Okay, glad you asked. Free speech is another emotionally charged topic that jams our awareness radar and contributes to suboptimal exchanges and connections. Allow me to explain.

The First Amendment right to free speech in the U.S. is not an absolute right. It does not protect the speaker from *all* retaliation or criticism. It only protects the speaker in the United States from U.S. government retaliation. Some countries don't even provide that much protection. Let that sink in a moment.

The distinction between government retaliation and all retaliation is often misunderstood. Many people assume free speech shields them from all consequences. That "free" means there is no cost associated with it, giving them an all-purpose pass to say whatever they want. Those folks are dead wrong. Free speech is always a calculated risk.

Managers are certainly entitled to their opinions and have a right to express them. When they use poor judgment in doing so, it *also* entitles them to a Pandora's box of consequences. Management does not get to uncouple the two. No one does. Free speech is never free. There is always a price to be paid, and it's better to determine those costs with foresight, not hindsight.

Words that negatively strike deep emotional chords have a radioactive shelf-life. It doesn't matter whether they're careless, knowingly offensive, or total lies flying under the flag of free speech. Those statements can be used against the speaker in a court of law and open the speaker to attack on social media. They can also be the basis for severing employment or creating separate legal liability for the organization. In some cases, low employee engagement may be the least of anyone's problems.

Indeed, many statements I've witnessed as an attorney were no doubt written or said in the heat of the moment, with false assumptions about privacy, and without a clue about how they could be interpreted negatively, or the consequences they could unleash. But once the sentiments are expressed, it's too late. The damage is done. Feelings are bruised, workplace relationships are injured, and trust is trampled.

When discourteous discourse breeds anger that boils over into lawsuits, those same free speech communications get a lot more expensive. They're now witness statements and potential smoking gun documents. They're evidence. They're Exhibit A.

Sadly, no one ever really wins a lawsuit. One side merely loses less. I say that because the cost of suing, or getting sued, in today's world is high for all involved. It's an emotional rollercoaster of high hopes dashed by procedural delays, the occasional reputation loss and tarnished career, plus the financial drain of endless legal bills while the case grinds slowly through the system. It's not at all like those TV courtroom dramas that reach a verdict in an hour, including commercials. The litigation process can take years, especially when drawn out by lengthy appeals. It can consume multiple budget cycles and rekindle anger, resentment, and frustration each time a new court deadline floats to the top of management's inbox.

In the meantime, employees who are attacked or disrespected in the name of free speech will disengage to varying degrees and take less ownership interest in their employ. Do they still care about their jobs? Sure, but not that much. Their withdrawal is a form of self-preservation.

FAIRNESS FACTOR

Fairness is about anticipating and balancing
the risk-reward tradeoffs of free speech.

The Biggest Consequence of Unfairly Using Positional Power

Over time the steady drip, drip, drip of disrespect in any shape or form, whether through politically incorrect statements or uninhibited free speech, weakens relationship bonds by eroding trust and goodwill. Connections get more stressed and frayed with each uncivil interaction, injecting more fear and resentment over being treated unfairly into the business ecosystem. When that happens, it usually takes more than one act of kindness for employees to have a reason to do more than show up at work.

One tech manager confessed his department head had a habit of taking the entire team to a fancy restaurant during business hours for a year-end holiday luncheon. "Sure," he said, "it was a nice gesture, but it didn't make up for the rest of the year when he was a total jerk." That response is no surprise. A token gesture does little to restore trust or goodwill when an employee's emotional bank account has been long overdrawn due to the norms nobody wants to talk about.

By the time organizations recognize they have an engagement problem, trust has been squandered and can't be force-fed with required retreats or artificial team-building exercises. Those activities can certainly be a good first step toward improving employee relationships, but they have their limits and should never be viewed as a total solution any more than the annual IT luncheon.

Employees are savvy. They recognize the difference between disguising and remedying unfairness. The unspoken questions employees want answered when such attempts are made are *What's really changed?* and *Why should we believe this now?*

Low trust represents a disconnect in any relationship. If we're talking about a casual acquaintance, it may not matter that much. If it's someone we need to rely on to get work done, it definitely does. Trust is a relationship shock absorber that makes saying "I'm sorry" or "That's not what I meant" believable, allowing people to seamlessly move on from misunderstandings or setbacks.

FAIRNESS FACTOR

Fairness is about sustaining trusting workplace relationships.

How we connect with others matters. Stephen M.R. Covey, author of *The Speed of Trust*, quantified how positive, collaborative, and uplifting communications accelerate business strategy and generate a 20% productivity dividend. Similarly, world-class communications contribute to a 40% increase thanks to the amazing energy produced by highly engaged employees. Trust thereby *expands* a leader's ability to get more done, in effect *increasing* their power and authority. Trust is reputational capital and pure gold.

In stark contrast, Covey finds organizations with guarded communications (low trust), or with intense micro-management and verbal, emotional, and/or physical abuse (nonexistent trust), experience a 60% and an 80% tax respectively. Indeed, when trust runs dry, it's immensely challenging to move day-to-day activities forward.

The impact on employee retention is also noteworthy. High-stakes headhunter Scott Love, author of *Why They Follow: How to Lead with Positive Influence*, explained during an interview with me for *Business Confidential Now* that he's had tens of thousands of recruiting conversations with professionals over two decades. When someone tells him they're not interested in exploring a more attractive opportunity he asks why. The answer is usually because they trust their boss, feel safe around them, and love where they are.

In comparison, when they *are* open to learning about a new job, he asks them what motivates them to make a change. The answer is hardly ever about pay or benefits he says. It's usually attributed to how leadership exercises their power. What Love hears most often is one or more of these statements:

"I don't trust them. I don't feel safe. I've seen people get passed over for all the wrong reasons. I've given ideas that are never heard. Our strategy is off. I've seen that the manager is putting his own career ahead of the company, and I just know what the end game is going to be with that."

For one reason or another, what these job candidates have seen, heard, and otherwise experienced has shattered their sense of good faith and fair dealing. It echoes my own experience with clients who leave employers, and/or sue, because frustration levels have reached a tipping point. Their reasonable expectations under the implied social contract have simply been crushed too often.

The challenge of any implied agreement, including the implied social contract, is identifying and understanding the unspoken expectations of the parties. The economic imbalance of power between the two in the workplace adds a wrinkle to the equation, requiring management to take the lead in keeping the relationship on track. The transformative nature of power, the belief of those in the driver's seat, that they're more right than anyone else, more exceptional, and more entitled to uninhibited expression, when left unchecked, creates an even bigger hurdle by amplifying that imbalance. It generates material disconnects with workers that have massive consequences for employee engagement and retention.

That disparity was vividly on display in two studies conducted by Hinge Research about the mid-career culture clash and talent crises service firms are experiencing. It revealed a stunning difference of opinion regarding employee satisfaction with organizational culture: 45% of senior management said they were satisfied compared to 17% of mid-career professionals.

Intrigued by these results, I interviewed Kelly Waffle, Hinge's Head of Digital Strategy, to learn more. "For some reason, once you cross over that threshold into senior leadership, the way that you look at things happens to change," he said. "Even though they'd been in that mid-career role at one time in their lives, they've seemed to have forgotten that."

Over a third of the employees surveyed by Hinge had left their jobs in the past year, and a significant number departed without another offer in hand. They were frustrated with their leadership teams, feeling senior management did not understand them and was out of touch. The lack of empathy reflected in these findings is palpable and sadly, the bigger the organization, the more frequent the disconnect between senior and mid-level managers.

> "We don't see things as they are, we see them as we are."
> ~Anaïs Nin (emphasis added)

Yes, workplace observations can differ dramatically depending on the box we occupy on the organizational chart. But it's the exercise of management power that determines whether the connections on the chart inspire self-motivation and discretionary effort or discourage it.

─────(FAIRNESS FACTOR)─────

Fairness is about using power equitably and responsibly.

What follows in Part Two of this book is a system of checks and balances to help executives, managers, and entrepreneurs infuse more fairness into their organization's culture to support more employee engagement and retention, to assist them in addressing the norms nobody wants to talk about; and to strengthen their organizational power by demonstrating more fairness.

The best performing companies, according to Gallup, have an employee engagement rate of 70% and on average experience 23% higher profits than those with actively disengaged employees. Imagine the untapped treasure trove of talent already on the payroll and the potential it represents for responsible leadership!

Time for another reality check and a recap of how power impacts the covenants of good faith and fair dealing of implied employee-employer contract and Maslow's Hierarchy of Human Motivational Needs and what it teaches us about the need for fairness at work:

✓ Fairness is about appreciating the pivotal role power plays in the implied social contract between employees and employers.

✓ Fairness is about exercising power consistent with the principles of good faith and fair dealing.

✓ Fairness is about awareness and empathy.

✓ Fairness is about kindness and being considerate of employee needs and fears.

✓ Fairness is about respecting the employees' point of view.

✓ Fairness is about remembering we're on the same team.

✓ Fairness is about exercising power respectfully.

✓ Fairness is about being open-minded.

✓ Fairness is about anticipating and balancing the risk-reward tradeoffs of free speech.

✓ Fairness is about sustaining trusting workplace relationships.

✓ Fairness is about using power equitably and responsibly.

Part

Two

A Five-Part Strategy for Improving Fairness at Work

Chapter 4

Rebuild Trust with More Self-Awareness

How power is used in organizations determines whether it unites us with trust or divides us with fear. Fairness plays a central role in that process because it's impossible to fully trust someone we believe is unfair. Fearful employees spend more time and energy looking over their shoulders and being defensive. In contrast, those who feel safe and have a strong sense of belonging can more easily stay focused on the organization's mission. As a result, the fairer someone is the more they can be trusted and the more they can raise their employees' game instead of defenses. There is no trust without fairness.

FAIRNESS FACTOR

Fairness is the foundation of trust.

Yet many leaders believe their positional power alone should command trust, that it's independent of individual relationships or behaviors and that it's automatically pre-packaged with respect for their role in the organization. While it's naïve to believe positional authority doesn't play an outsized role in workplace relationships, it's also hasty to assume it is the sole factor determining trust. It's not.

The ability to truly lead depends on *legitimacy* of power, not mere positional power, and that legitimacy or influence cannot be assumed. It requires emotional consent. It must be earned by demonstrating integrity. This is precisely where the implied social contract comes into play, along with its covenants of good faith and fair dealing. Fairness and trust are about justice.

Part of the challenge when talking about trust and fairness is that *our* truth colors our perceptions of what's fair. Our awareness is one-sided. It's only by garnering employees' perspectives that management can begin to understand workers' expectations under the implied social contract and can begin to appreciate why certain management behaviors stand in the way of trust.

FAIRNESS FACTOR

Fairness is about understanding the employees' point of view
and expectations under the implied social contract.

Yeah, we're one step ahead of you here. Our company does employee engagement and satisfaction surveys, so we're aware of what employees are thinking and their point of view.

Surveys, Surveys, Surveys

Surveys are great! Discovering different perspectives and why they matter help us identify ways to improve relationships damaged by the norms nobody wants to talk about. It deepens our understanding of how others see the world and allows us to grasp how their decisions, intentions, and beliefs may be legitimately different from our own. The purpose of acquiring such information should not be to make one person right at the expense of another, but rather to open our minds to other narratives and inspire ways to reconcile different expectations.

"Sunlight is said to be the best of disinfectants."
~JUSTICE LOUIS BRANDEIS

An array of assessment tools is available to assist management in learning about employees' workplace experiences and point of view. Traditional employee engagement surveys, for example, are used to measure emotional commitment and are often supplemented with satisfaction surveys aimed at determining whether employees are happy and believe they're being treated fairly.

Unfortunately, those surveys are often administered infrequently, making them a single snapshot in time that can suffer from the Santa Halo Effect. Just as children anticipating a visit from St. Nick will be on good behavior and play nice, some managers have been known to be on their best behavior before survey time in an effort to favorably skew the results. As soon as the scores are tallied, they slide back to their old habits, and nothing really changes, except hoodwinked employees get more disillusioned and cynical.

Forward-thinking companies, recognizing the shortcomings of such assessment tools and the fact that employee morale and workplace culture are dynamic, have gone further in recent years, implementing pulse surveys that are more flexible and administered more frequently. Workplace culture has a rhythm and a flow. It breathes. To ferret out what's really going on requires more than an annual check-up.

Pulse surveys are more comprehensive and seek workers' views about the entire employee lifecycle, including onboarding, diversity, inclusion, well-being, training and development, and more. The goal is to provide continuous, real-time feedback to management. The belief that frequency will promote more leadership accountability and positive change has made them popular. But even pulse surveys can fall short and suffer from the same drawbacks that plague the effectiveness and value of any other engagement and satisfaction survey.

Survey Design

Survey design is critical. Knowing *what* to ask employees and *how* to ask it is essential regardless of what survey method is used. Superficial queries lead to perfunctory answers. To extract more insights, especially in an environment where employees fear retaliation, asking about what's happening instead of what's wrong can indirectly reveal truths about whether workers are respected, appreciated, coached, developed, or cared about as people. Such questions are good faith and fair dealing yardsticks whose answers can expose cultural landmines hiding in plain view that employees might otherwise be too afraid to say out loud.

FAIRNESS FACTOR

Fairness is about asking the right questions
to identify the root cause of problems.

A well-designed and well-executed workforce review can reveal powerful information about the health of an organization's culture. But those data points should never be confused with creating better employee engagement any more than weighing oneself is all that's needed to achieve a healthy weight. It's merely one data point and the beginning of a multi-step process.

Survey Follow-up

Management needs to be transparent about survey results: the good, the bad, and the ugly. Appropriate follow-up is essential because lack of management ownership is a huge morale killer.

Some companies address this issue head-on by sharing the negative scores they receive with employees and then confidentially continuing the conversation one-on-one with individual workers to learn more. It lets the person know they've been heard, explains what steps will be taken to address and remedy sticking points, and by when. If possible, future feedback includes actual progress that's been made to let workers know the corner offices are taking their concerns seriously.

Even if management decides to maintain the status quo, explaining why no change will be implemented can open the door to dialogue and go a long way toward employee acceptance. Either way, closing the feedback loop with employees is preferable to closing the door because including them in the conversation supports their sense of belonging.

———{ FAIRNESS FACTOR }———

Fairness is about honestly sharing employee
engagement survey results and next steps.

Rejecting Survey Results

Management may challenge the validity of its employee survey results, either dismissing them as the product of a few rogue employees (even when statistically the numbers don't support that conclusion) or insisting on finding out who was responsible for the "bad marks" so they can retaliate. This response shuts down the psychological safety necessary for honest communication. It promotes a culture of fear, and the next time employees receive surveys asking for their opinions, they'll tell management what they want to hear instead of the truth— even in "anonymous" surveys.

For employees, surveys create a presumption that their opinions and point of view matter. But when results get buried and nothing changes, or worse yet if they're retaliated against, it leads them to conclude their beliefs are outliers. It sends a message that they need to obey and conform, reinforcing the norms nobody wants to talk about and increasing perceptions of unfairness at work.

In the short term it crushes dissent. But silence doesn't mean acceptance. It's brought about by subtle forms of coercion and intimidation, not because the norms nobody wants to talk about have been remedied or employee expectations of good faith and fair dealing have been met. As a result, employee dissatisfaction continues and complaints go underground.

———{ FAIRNESS FACTOR }———

Fairness is about accepting employee engagement
survey results, not retaliating.

Asking the human resources department to handle survey fallout and fix problems creates the illusion that management is taking responsibility for organizational culture. Those professionals can certainly help mediate and provide counsel regarding misunderstandings and disputes between employees and their supervisors. But, only the parties themselves can make meaningful changes to their workplace relationship. It's something they need to do themselves. Relationships can't be delegated.

FAIRNESS FACTOR

Fairness is about management taking ownership
of employee survey results and workplace relationships.

Power, Surveys, and Fairness

Surveys are nice, but they're ultimately no match for the unbridled use of management power. Leaders who discount the accuracy of survey results or who outsource accountability for them to human resources exhibit some of the ugly power dynamics explored in Chapter 3. They protect their self-image and interests at the expense of the best interests of the organization. Flexing their muscle this way is inconsistent with good asset stewardship.

FAIRNESS FACTOR

Fairness is about using power responsibly, with good faith
and fair dealing, and in the best interests of the organization.

Just as performance reviews shouldn't surprise employees, engagement and satisfaction survey results shouldn't shock management. Poor communication and inattentiveness to how their actions contribute to unpalatable situations cause supervisors to be blindsided, as illustrated in the following example.

Case of the Surprise Resignation

The sharp knock on the executive vice president's door announced the arrival of one of his direct reports, a high performer and 10-year employee. She handed him a piece of paper. The document was short. His jaw dropped as he read it in disbelief and bewilderment. It was her resignation.

"You're not serious, are you?" He paused, reread the letter, then looked up. "I have to go to my executive leadership meeting now, let's talk about this later."

"Yes, I am serious. And no, there's nothing to talk about. What for?" she replied. "We haven't really talked in years. What's the point?"

When he shared news of her resignation with the CEO and rest of the senior leadership team, he was chided. "You just let your best employee leave," one of them said.

The colleague who resigned later discovered her supervisor confided in an associate that he knew she wasn't happy but didn't know what to do. He was afraid to ask for help from human resources because he thought it would make him look weak. So, he did nothing. Besides, in his opinion the employee's age left her with limited job options. He never dreamed she'd quit before reaching official retirement age. Age bias clouded his thinking.

The fact that they hadn't really talked in years and the employee thought there was no point in starting spoke volumes about the lack of trust in this workplace relationship. Unfortunately for the executive vice president, doing nothing did not preserve the status quo. It made things worse by allowing problems to fester. More self-awareness and better conflict management skills on his part might have changed the outcome and avoided the loss of talent.

Self-Awareness, Influence, and Trust

I appreciate how self-awareness is an unsettling concept for some and why they bristle at its mere mention. It can be scary to look in the mirror. It's deeply personal because our own insecurities make us afraid of what we might see. Instead of saying, *tell me more,* the instinctive impulse is to get defensive, avoid introspection, and dodge uncomfortable feedback. In contrast, the best leaders embrace personal growth and change.

Genuine trust is an emotional connection, not a transactional one, and greater self-awareness increases our ability to generate it by helping us identify the self-defeating behaviors we may not realize we engage in that get in the way. It thereby opens the door to stronger emotional connections, making us more relatable, easier to work with, and better equipped to build high-performance business cultures.

"If you really want to lead others, if you want to really exercise influence over [employees]," says Professor Sim Sitkin of the Duke University Fuqua School of Business, "you've got to have a sense of yourself, and you've got to have a sense of how you're connecting with others." What it all means for executives, managers, and entrepreneurs is that gaining more self-awareness can reduce team dysfunction and help raise everyone's game. It paves the way for better workplace relationships and more employee engagement.

Sitkin says there are three types of self-awareness essential to successful business leadership:

1. a leader's awareness of their internal state – their beliefs, values, emotions, and physical feelings

2. a leader's awareness of their external state – their physical appearance, how they dress, their demeanor, their poise, and how they communicate

3. a leader's social awareness – an appreciation and understanding of how they're being perceived by others

"Sometimes, being a very strong authority figure means you're basically not paying any attention to how other people are seeing you. You're just doing what you want to do," he says.

─────┤ FAIRNESS FACTOR ├─────
Fairness is about utilizing self-awareness to
appreciate how we impact someone else's point of view.

Unfortunately, such general self-awareness, or emotional intelligence as it's also called, gets dismissed in business circles as a soft skill unbefitting a hard-charging results-oriented leader or business owner.

The capacity for self-awareness is more valuable than many realize because the intense pressure and stress management works under creates a laser focus on the bottom line. It's an uncompromised level of concentration that unwittingly distracts them and blinds them to hot-button behaviors they've internalized as acceptable. Ironically, these behaviors have been tolerated by the organization in the past and have diminished trust in the workplace—the very trust they need to succeed.

As a result, leaders need to know "where they hold and where they fold" says executive coach Jill Ratliff, author of *Leadership Through Trust & Collaboration*. They need to appreciate how their behaviors negatively affect those around them. Instead of exploding in anger or frustration when they're disappointed, for example, a smarter approach is to take a moment and identify exactly why they're upset. What expectation has been left unmet? How was that expectation communicated to employees? Was it explicit, or implicit? How were employees supposed to know?

> *"The single biggest problem with communication*
> *is the illusion that it has taken place."*
> ~ GEORGE BERNARD SHAW

Ratliff's simple exercise helps develop more internal self-awareness and helps zero in on what prompts the supervisor's emotional response. Self-regulation then lets managers redirect their energy into joint problem solving *regardless* of who is right or wrong she says. It effectively changes the conversation from "you have a problem" to "we have a problem." Now, let's figure out how we fix it *together*.

FAIRNESS FACTOR

Fairness is about having more self-awareness
of our interactions and impact on others.

That last part can be hard for some leaders. Their fears, ego, and/or cocoon of positional power make it difficult for them to not insist on being right and making someone else wrong. Indeed, as previously discussed in Chapter 3, the very nature of having power can heighten an individual's confidence and perceptions of exceptionalism, blinding them to their own fallibility or even the merits or legitimacy of someone else's viewpoint.

Rising Above the Fear of Being Taken Advantage of

But what if I'm too nice? I could lose control. Reminding people who is in charge by injecting a little fear now and then, such as joking about the ability to fire them keeps them from taking advantage of me. It can be a good thing. Heh-heh. No?

Flirting with talk of indiscriminate separation is never funny to those within earshot who have less power or influence to defend themselves. They already know an at-will work environment means they can be separated from their jobs for any reason at any time. Firing reminders casually tossed around like confetti to celebrate power are deeply unsettling and stressful because they're intensely memorable and undermine trust in a prolonged way.

Stressful? Memorable? I'm just kidding . . . it's a joke. Give me a break! Where's your sense of humor?

Research by neuroscientist Dr. James L. McGaugh shows how *any* type of emotional arousal, both good and bad, can create lasting memories. This is why people remember where they were when hearing tragic news, such as the attack on the World Trade Center in New York City or the death of a loved one, and vividly recall special moments such as their first kiss. Mundane events, on the other hand, those that don't trigger our emotions are easily forgotten.

What we recall and how graphically we remember it depends on the emotional significance of the event. Dr. McGaugh's research finds long-term memory consolidation occurs when the adrenal stress hormones epinephrine and corticosterone get triggered and the amygdala plays a major role in that process. That's why employees won't forget the details of stinging criticism from their manager, career ending "jokes," or behaviors that betray the covenants of good faith and fair dealing.

Threats get seared into the memory of those being attacked because the amygdala is where the brain processes threatening stimuli. Yet for supervisors who regularly engage in such comic relief the remarks could be more of a blur, if not forgotten altogether. They could even be flatly denied as ever happening because it's simply not emotionally significant or memorable for them. It doesn't threaten *them*, so it's not baked into their memory banks the way it is for employees.

Stop and think about this memory consolidation process for a moment. If emotions help us remember what's significant, because that's how human brains are wired, wouldn't leveraging positive emotions instead of negative ones be a much smarter way to forge better workplace connections? To build trust? To ignite more employee commitment? Of course it would.

One method Ratliff uses to help leaders identify their emotional hot buttons is by inviting them to keep track of all the challenging things that happen during the day for a week. It helps bring to the surface their *subconscious* reactions she says and creates a more *conscious* awareness of what triggers them. Once managers recognize those patterns it can be followed up with new behaviors to respond in a smarter, more positive, way that reflects empathy.

Bringing Positive Energy into the Room

Great business leaders take responsibility for bringing positive energy to workplace relationships and for creating that same sense of safety and trust Scott Love heard about in his recruiting calls that generate loyalty and a resounding, *no thanks—I love it here.*

We've all heard winning sports teams thank their fans for the raucous cheers propelling them to victory and heard stage performers buoyed by audience applause express their gratitude. It's all due to the positive energy in the room. It signals support and generates momentum. It's energy transference, and it's something we perceive intuitively. We experience how contagious it can be on a personal level when meeting people who radiate warmth and enthusiasm, as well as the buzzkills who drain our emotional battery with their boorish demeanor and behavior.

It took neuroscientist Jill Bolte Taylor recovering from a stroke on the left side of her brain to validate how our brains process this phenomenon. Taylor is the author of *My Stroke of Insight* and writes how her tragic condition robbed her of the left-brained reasoning and analytic skills we use to decipher language. To compensate, the intuitive right-brained side took over, and despite being unconscious she could sense the positive or negative energy of her visitors. She also noticed how those vibes affected her healing process, either enabling or hindering her progress depending on the nature of the energy.

The same phenomenon occurs in the workplace. Each morning executives, managers, and entrepreneurs have a choice about what kind of energy they project when speaking with employees. The air can crackle with the excitement of possibilities or be thick with despair. It's up to them.

───────(FAIRNESS FACTOR)───────

Fairness is about bringing positive energy into the room.

Look, it's unrealistic to expect me to be "Susie Sunshine" all the time. Actually, I'm not even sure I can do that part of the time. I have a right to my anger and frustration. This job isn't easy you know!

You're right. Leadership responsibilities are significant, and managers are entitled to their feelings. But scaring people with threatening, volatile, or retaliatory behavior doesn't create a trusting culture where people are self-motivated to do their best work. They'll be too afraid to make a mistake and be taken to task in an unforgiving way. They'll play it safe instead. It's tough to accelerate business growth when employees feel the need to keep the emergency brake on due to suboptimal leadership.

Getting Smarter Requires Embracing Humility

Managers who are able to embrace humility can strengthen their leadership capabilities and self-awareness by recognizing their title doesn't make them omnipotent or give them all the answers. Actually, managers don't really need to have the answers. What they do need is to engage more with others, to ask the right questions of the right people, to listen deeply, and to learn from those around them. That process can yield huge dividends. It can help build trust, increase employees' sense of belonging and esteem, as well as help generate the best solutions to allow leaders to make more informed decisions.

───────(FAIRNESS FACTOR)───────

Fairness is about exercising humility to engage with others
to build trust, increase employees' sense of belonging, generate
the best solutions, and make more informed decisions.

Humbly accepting feedback and subordinating our ego transforms conversations from "I" to "we" according to Warren Rustand, Dean of Learning for Entrepreneurs Organization, Global Leadership Academy. "We need people close to us that we trust who are willing to tell us the truth and sometimes we have our sphere of people around us, our entourage, and they're yes-people." The more honest and truthful the feedback we receive about how what we do impacts others, the more self-awareness we're able to develop, and the more knowledgeable we become about how to build more trusting workplace relationships.

Okay, I get it. But in the grand scheme of things, what is MY self-awareness going to do to help improve employee engagement and retention?

Connection Between Self-Awareness and Good Faith and Fair Dealing

Self-awareness helps us appreciate how we may be contributing to the norms nobody wants to talk about and eroding trust in our workplace relationships. Immediate supervisors play a particularly outsized role in how employees feel about their employer according to Gallup research detailed in the book *It's the Manager*. Their relationship style influences the workplace norms employees experience every day. Managers assign work, provide direction, evaluate performance, influence raises, champion promotions, and for all practical purposes *are* the employer.

Those norms, you may recall from Chapter 2, commonly fall into 5 categories: unapproachability, lack of recognition, bias, poor conflict management, and poor workload management. They betray employees' expectations of good faith and fair dealing in multiple ways, causing them to bring less discretionary effort to the job and commitment to the organization. Greater self-awareness can help us reverse that downward engagement spiral in multiple ways.

Better external self-awareness, as illustrated in Figure 4.1 next page, helps us appreciate how our communications and our demeanor impact our approachability and ability to manage conflict. Small adjustments in behavior can sometimes make a big difference in whether we're viewed as being fair and acting in good faith and with fair dealing.

	Self-Awareness
Unapproachability	
Unavailability	How
Ignoring/Shunning	We Present
Lack of Empathy	Ourselves
Lack of Recognition	
Wage Theft	
Timely Compensation	How We're
Subjective Rewards	Perceived
Credit Stealing	
No Feedback	
Bias	
Microaggressions	
Bullying	Our Internal
Discrimination	Values and
Harassment	Beliefs
Poor Conflict Management	
Volatility	How
Conflict Avoidance	We Present
Gaslighting	Ourselves
Retaliation	
Poor Workload Management	
Unclear Communications	
Micromanaging	How We're
Unrealistic Goals	Perceived
Lack of Support	

Figure 4.1 How Self-Awareness Can Address the Norms Nobody Wants to Talk About

Similarly, greater social self-awareness, the ability to observe and track how our messages are being received, is invaluable for avoiding misunderstandings about recognition and workload management. It's powerful because it gives us the opportunity to follow up with more information to clear up any confusion. It helps manage expectations and remedy unhelpful conduct that detracts from employees' sense of belonging.

Internal self-awareness is perhaps the most challenging for management to embrace. Yet it's incredibly important because our core beliefs, values, and emotions are reflected as bias that surfaces in our communications and influences the energy in the room. Their impact on employees' sense of belonging and self-motivation is also enormous. A 2019 inclusion barrier study conducted by Deloitte LLP found nearly two-thirds of the employees surveyed said they experienced or witnessed bias in the workplace within the past year, and 61% reported it happened at least once a month.

In sum, a candid sense of internal, external, and social self-awareness makes leaders more mindful and fully present when interacting with employees. It opens the door to better communications and stronger workplace relationships.

Before moving on to the next chapter and exploring communication chemistry, let's recap the fairness factors related to trust building that influence perceptions of good faith and fair dealing and what they can teach us about improving employee engagement, retention, and satisfaction:

- ✓ Fairness is the foundation of trust.

- ✓ Fairness is about understanding the employees' point of view and expectations under the implied social contract.

- ✓ Fairness is about asking the right questions to identify the root cause of problems.

- ✓ Fairness is about honestly sharing employee engagement survey results and next steps.

- ✓ Fairness is about accepting employee engagement survey results, not retaliating.

✓ Fairness is about management taking ownership of employee survey results and workplace relationships.

✓ Fairness is about using power responsibly, in good faith and with fair dealing, and in the best interests of the organization.

✓ Fairness is about utilizing self-awareness to appreciate how we impact someone else's point of view.

✓ Fairness is about having more self-awareness of our interactions and impact on others.

✓ Fairness is about bringing positive energy into the room.

✓ Fairness is about exercising humility to engage with others to build trust, increase employees' sense of belonging, generate the best solutions, and make more informed decisions.

Chapter 5

Improve Relationship Chemistry
with More Empathy

Empathy is essential to fairness at work. It humanizes conversations, promotes a sense of belonging, and affects the energy in the room. Empathy is relationship glue, unlike apathy, which is the mother of the norms nobody wants to talk about.

We're drawn to those who understand our perspective, who "get" us. It's a degree of connection that enables us to work *with* people who understand us, instead of merely *for* them, and that higher level of commitment translates into more employee engagement. In his book *The War for Kindness*, Stanford neuroscientist Jamil Zaki makes a strong case for the power of empathy, saying it not only improves connection with the person being accepted through understanding, it also benefits the person expressing it because signaling acceptance improves our *collective* sense of belonging. It brings more positive energy into the room. As a result, it pays to be kind.

Communication Styles

We've all met people with whom we've had an immediate connection, someone with whom it's easy to share information and ideas because their communication style makes us feel comfortable and safe. They are tolerant and listen without judgment. They're genuinely interested in our opinions. They know how to express sincere appreciation and their presence is reassuring because they encourage us with curiosity and enthusiasm. Their resourcefulness also gives us a safety net in times of need. They're supportive, even if it means telling us things that we don't want to hear because they do so constructively, not disparagingly. We know they're rooting for us by their overall behavior.

Written, verbal, and non-verbal messages communicate far more than mere facts and figures. Even omissions, those awkward pauses, silences, and gaps between our exchanges have meaning. Take too long to reply to a text or an email and the sender might jump to negative conclusions. Fail to take action altogether and it can leave people feeling abandoned. Every bit of how we convey information has meaning and significance apart from words alone. These communication cues can make us feel valued or shake us to our core.

Unfortunately, people often perceive empathy as a single, monolithic thing. It's not. Empathy is the art of combining attentiveness, respect, listening, self-regulation, compassion, curiosity, gratitude, and a growth mindset to build trust. It's determined by the totality of how we communicate and it requires humility, honesty, and consistency.

Analyzing how empathy is expressed and especially how it's perceived offers insight on how to improve our own communication skills to build the trust that empowers and supports self-motivated employees and makes them want to be part of our team.

OK, but isn't how we express ourselves just a matter of style?

Of course, our method of how we interact with others is who we are and how we express our unique personality. Being true to ourselves is part of being authentic, and at first blush the thought of changing how we communicate feels unnatural. Yet, everyone's style is automatically variable according to Dr. Deborah Tannen, a renowned professor of linguistics at Georgetown University.

Language is a shared means of communication, and we naturally adjust in response to the context and style of others in the group.

Such modifications are a normal part of how we connect with people. Far from being inauthentic, wanting others to understand our ideas, thoughts, and feelings shows we care. It's really a form of respect for the relationship, the foundation of trust, and the key to advancing a sense of belonging. As a result, identifying even small ways we can adjust our own technique and style puts us on a stronger path toward more workplace collaboration, productivity, and harmony.

Communication Rituals

Communication styles are composed of rituals according to Dr. Tannen. We use words to convey information, and it is the rituals that send meta-messages about our attitude toward the relationship. In many ways, they play an important role in how we wield power and the type of energy in the room. They set the tone, a key factor in establishing empathy.

Meta-messages include how we pace our speech. Do we speak *fast?* Or . . . more . . . slowly . . . and . . . deliberately? How often do we pause while speaking, and what is the duration of our pauses? The pregnant pause might give someone time to digest information, yet it can also be viewed as inviting others to join the conversation. Other signals or devices contributing to style are pitch, volume, and intonation.

Take for example the simple word "oh." It becomes a question when we turn our voice up at the end. It becomes judgmental when the first part of the word is louder and elongated when our voice drops lower at the end. And when said in a monotone "oh," it's a filler that can signal "go on," or even boredom. These minor changes can totally change its meaning. Try it.

Who knew such a tiny word could be a complete and powerful sentence? Right?

Now let's add body language (facial expressions, posture, hand gestures, and eye contact) plus a string of words that are more complex and subject to interpretation than "oh." It's easy to see how quickly misunderstandings can occur, especially when words are blurted out in anger.

> *"I've learned that people will forget what you said, people will forget what you did, but people will never forget how you made them feel."*
> ~MAYA ANGELOU

Non-verbal behaviors are particularly powerful. Research by Wharton Professor of Management Sigal Barsade confirms the ability of people in a work group to internalize what others around them are feeling by interpreting the energy generated through their body language: their facial expression, posture, and eye contact. Those cues contribute to energy transference. It's how we learned to interpret the world as babies well before developing any verbal skills. Even as adults, ninety percent of our message is transmitted non-verbally according to Dr. Helen Reiss, author of *The Empathy Effect*. It's no wonder we're more inclined to remember how people make us feel instead of what they said.

Unlike trained actors, most of us do not have the benefit of a script or coaching in the nuances of timing, inflection, tone, and facial expression or body language when delivering our lines. Life comes at us fast and unpredictably, forcing us to ad lib. When we're less prepared, we're more inclined to speak from an emotional place than when we're engaging in presentations, interviews or other critical conversations we've rehearsed.

As a result, we often subconsciously use the signals and devices that define our communication style without realizing or anticipating the impact they have on others. That lack of self-awareness is precisely why it's not uncommon for unrehearsed conversation rituals in the workplace to collide between co-workers and have unintended consequences.

Take for example the person who talks a mile a minute, who wildly interrupts, and verbally barrels over others. In some circles such patterns could be viewed as expressing enthusiasm or interest while others may see the same conduct as totally obnoxious. In exasperation, the person being interrupted might say *Pleeeease let me finish*. To them the constant interruptions signal the other person isn't listening, that they're being disrespectful.

If the fast talker doesn't adjust their style, voices will continually get louder as each person tries to drown out the other to be heard. That dynamic might work for certain TV pundits who believe they score points by interrupting and verbally stepping on each other's lines, but in the workplace that method doesn't advance the conversation. It's stifling. It's staticky. It's domineering and can be viewed as bullying. It leaves participants feeling exhausted, dispirited, and misunderstood.

The fact that a single conversation ritual can be viewed in opposite ways emphasizes how easily a speaker's intent can be eclipsed by alternate interpretations. Doubling down on a particular communication style because someone flexes their leadership muscle and thinks they're right only makes things worse. It's as effective as the American in Paris who thinks repeating their question louder in English will help a French person understand.

Reconciling Conflicting Communication Styles

When people draw conclusions opposite from what the speaker intends it's usually due to conflicting styles says Dr. Tannen. That's not to say one type is better than another. Each is equally valid and has its own logic. They're also culturally relative: we're influenced by our families, ethnicity, gender, education, past experiences, and even regional geographic differences. What that means for leaders is that unifying these differences rather than rejecting them out of hand is the path to better team collaboration and employee engagement.

FAIRNESS FACTOR

Fairness is about reconciling communication styles
and tone to improve connection.

Oh, come on! Now I need to watch not only what I say, but what everybody else says. This is crazy. Why is it my responsibility to navigate all these diverse communication styles? It sounds like a mine field.

Yeah, and when you think of it like that, it sure is. Navigating suggests we're trying to find ways around someone's style—to bypass or override it, or find an escape hatch. But if instead we view management's role as uniting employees in furtherance of the organization's mission, the leadership responsibility crystalizes into how we can harmonize diverse communication styles in a way that benefits the organization.

Think of it as leading an orchestra. Each instrument lends texture, richness, and beauty to the whole. It's the leader's role as the conductor to allow each voice to be heard and contribute their best thinking in a coordinated fashion. By asking for clarification or more information to help avoid misunderstandings before they turn into resentment, the organization can profit from employees' collective wisdom. Better meeting management is one area that could benefit from such synchronization. Allowing employees to be heard and understood opens the door to diverse points of view and helps identify new possibilities. It's the essence of collaboration and employee engagement.

Okay, I understand what you're saying about communication styles and these rituals. But we're not always in the same room. More employees are working remotely than ever before. How am I supposed to bring energy into a virtual "room?"

Meeting the Challenge of Remote Communications

Great question. It's one that I posed during my podcast interview with Dr. Diane Lennard, Professor of Management Communication at the NYU Stern School of Business and co-author of *Humanizing the Remote Experience Through Leadership and Coaching*. She faces the exact same issue when teaching her students through video conferencing and makes an extra effort to promote psychological safety and a sense of belonging by compensating for missing social cues.

"One of the things that the brain does is predict people's behavior and intentions by reading verbal and nonverbal signals," says Lennard. Those are missing in remote environments, making communication more challenging. To counterbalance that deficiency, we need to focus more on our verbal skills she says. "Sometimes we have to be more explicit when we're talking. We also have to put more priority on the person asking somebody to speak rather than allowing people to disappear and not have a voice."

Computer screens only capture the upper body on screen and important body language often gets lost. If during face-to-face meetings managers usually rely on non-verbal cues such as hand gestures and subtle head nods to convey approval or signal someone else's turn to speak, verbalizing those same thoughts will make remote communications more successful. Specifically calling on people to contribute instead of letting them hide behind a screen lets them know that management values their capabilities and is open to their ideas.

"Getting each person to talk is extremely important for building psychological safety and trust. You want to get as many voices into the conversation as possible [and] create a nonjudgmental environment," she says. People need to feel safe, to understand others, and to have a sense of belonging. "Sharing is a key part of this, as is empathy," she claims. It humanizes the remote communication experience when we use words carefully to gather information, clearly express expectations about work product and deadlines, and confirm our shared understanding; as well as connecting by mutually sharing our feelings, goals, motivation, and availability.

Following those best practices benefit any meeting and take on greater significance in the virtual world because our brains work harder to understand what's going on in the absence of nonverbal cues. Having less information to work with is stressful.

Written communications face the same need for clarity remote conferencing does. The more casual the writing, the greater the opportunity for misunderstanding. Unlike formal reports, memos, and letters that have the benefit of review, reflection, and editing; text messages and email sent in the heat of the moment don't. They're spontaneous and less filtered. Although they may feel private, they're not.

—————(FAIRNESS FACTOR)—————
Fairness in remote electronic conferencing and
written communications is about striving for clarity and
compensating for missing verbal and visual cues.

Going Viral

A chief drawback of electronic communication is the unwanted attention and national publicity it can create due to its capacity for mass distribution of embarrassing messages with a single click. Such was the case for office and home furniture maker Miller Knoll's CEO, Andi Owen. Her recorded town hall comments became the subject of viral criticism when in response to a question about how employees can stay motivated if they're not paid bonuses, she admonished them to leave "pity city" and focus instead on achieving higher sales.

The CEO of digital marketing and advertising firm Clearlink, James Clarke, faced the same problem when during his virtual town hall about a return to office mandate he challenged employee loyalty and work ethic by accusing some of them of "quiet quitting." He also insulted working moms by claiming it's rare for them to be successful caregivers and productive full-time employees while he simultaneously praised the worker who sold her family dog so she could physically return to the office. Both CEOs later apologized in response to the massive public backlash they received to their tone-deaf comments.

When dealing with large virtual meetings, it's wise to heed the advice of Ed Barks, a high-powered Washington, D.C. communications strategy and training consultant, and former member of the National Press Club's Board of Governors. He says leaders should focus on three things:

1. testing and staying on message to make sure it consistently conveys what they really want

2. honing their technique to rein in the non-verbal cues that detract from their message

3. monitoring their attitude to keep from being combative and treating the audience as the enemy.

Although my conversation with Barks centered on media interviews, his sage advice applies equally to large virtual meetings where the audience is often out of sight, their feelings are easily neglected, and getting everyone to participate is not physically possible.

Barks' third point, about staying on message and avoiding combativeness is terrific advice for any type of communication, including written ones. Emails and text messages can go viral too, especially when shared on social media. In my experience it's usually the gasp-worthy snarky tone of those communications, their "Oh my gosh, I can't believe they said that" quality, that causes the most harm because they deeply offend our expectations of civility.

> **FAIRNESS FACTOR**
> Fairness is about keeping workplace communications professional.

Each communication channel has its strengths and weaknesses and leaders interested in building trust are well advised to utilize the medium best suited to protecting their messages and their workplace relationships. Efficiency and convenience must always be weighed against the potential for collateral damage. Doing something because management can doesn't mean they necessarily should. Using electronic media, for example, to swing the axe and announce layoffs may be fast and sidestep emotional face-to-face meetings, but it's cowardly. It sends a chilling message to the rest of the workforce that damages perceptions of good faith and fair dealing because it is not necessary to be cruel or indifferent when conducting layoffs. Being attentive to employees' needs means finding ways to achieve business objectives in more respectful and compassionate way.

> **FAIRNESS FACTOR**
> Fairness is about choosing and using communication channels wisely.

Avoiding Old Habits

It takes practice, and it takes time to avoid falling into old habits and responding swiftly in the heat of the moment. Nonetheless, it's important not to react and allow our amygdala to emotionally hijack our decision-making process says Steven Howard, author of *Better Decisions, Better Thinking, Better Outcomes*. Leaders can exercise more self-control when they feel their temperature rising if they count to eight.

Seriously? Eight? What's so great about the number eight?

Simple. It's science.

Magnetic resonance imaging scans of the brain (MRIs) show it takes approximately eight seconds for the prefrontal cortex, the area of the brain responsible for executive function and impulse moderation, to take over from the amygdala. We can count to ten to give us extra time to stop us from saying or doing something we'll later regret, or we can sleep on it overnight, or even take a walk. The point is to buy time. When faced with news that sets off our internal alarms, we can simply say we'll think about it. Do whatever it takes to give the prefrontal cortex a chance to boot up and do its job.

The benefit of reflection is the opportunity it gives us to formulate a less emotional response, to make sure it's proportional, measured, reasonable, and demonstrates good faith. Doing so helps build trust and burnish our reputation as a leader employees want to work with because we're fair.

Emotional volatility, on the other hand, is toxic. It provokes fear and sends people diving for cover. No one wants to be in the line of fire of a supervisor who is yelling or cursing. The emotional shockwave it sends through the organization threatens our sense of physical and psychological safety. It spectacularly fails to promote any sense of belonging.

FAIRNESS FACTOR

Fairness is about emotional self-regulation.

Compassion, Listening, and Curiosity

Okay, I admit that I sometimes get upset with my employees. But there is only so much whining and complaining I can deal with.

I appreciate how productivity demands, financial burdens, and the stress of day-to-day leadership contribute to compassion fatigue. After a while we get tired of hearing about repetitive problems or difficult issues. But let's not forget that problem-solving is an important management responsibility. If organizations didn't have problems and challenges, they wouldn't need leaders.

The solution to compassion fatigue is for managers to catch their breath and take a break to recharge their own emotional batteries. Their feelings may seem private to them, but their outlook subconsciously colors everything they say and do. Those emotions are more visible to employees than many in power realize. That's why self-awareness is so valuable and important to building and sustaining strong relationships.

Compassion fatigue can be a potent petri dish for the norms nobody wants to talk about. Its symptoms can appear as indifference to problems and/or shunning the people who raise them, and even blaming them for it—a tactic also known as "shooting the messenger." The lack of empathy it represents can manifest itself further in delayed decision-making, being unavailable to employees, and failing to support them with timely information, resources, and/or realistic goals. When challenged about such short-comings management frustration can lead to lashing out, playing the positional power card, and compounding the problem by doubling down.

With self-regulation, however, leaders can demonstrate more compassion by actively listening, being curious and genuinely interested in what employees think about the projects, problems, and/or issues needing to be solved. Hearing employees out doesn't mean leaders necessarily agree or are abdicating their decision-making authority. It's merely information gathering and taking steps to understand other points of view before making management's own thoughts known. Think of it as a learning opportunity.

------(**FAIRNESS FACTOR**)------
Fairness is about making time to actively
listen and learn without judgment.

Listening to Learn

Unfortunately, listening is an often underappreciated and underutilized skill. "We can think in a much faster rate than a person can speak, so it gives us extra time. If we do get off track or think about something else, we can really lose out on the conversation and valuable information," says Dr. Kittie Watson, listening expert and author of the book *Listen Up.*

Exercising empathy and especially self-regulation can be challenging when we hear information we disagree with. That's what happened to Sarita Maybin after she attended a supervisor training session where it was recommended managers ask their staff for suggestions on how to improve their one-on-one meetings. When she returned to the office, she followed their advice and asked one of the people she supervised about his opinions. His response stunned her. "You could be a better supervisor," he said.

In recounting the story Maybin said "red alert alarms" were going off in her head when she heard his feedback. Her first instinct was to shut down his insubordination. *How dare he challenge her authority and supervisory ability!* But then she remembered what a graduate school mentor advised when faced with criticism: "Ask for more," he counseled. So, she did.

Maybin became curious. She asked him to elaborate, to provide details and examples. At the end of the conversation, he noted the team really didn't know how well they were doing on a day-to-day basis. It would help them if during their meetings she told them one thing they were good at and the one thing they need to improve.

That piece of advice was a game changer. Maybin called it brilliant, and it truly is. It's easy to take for granted the things that are progressing the way they should, but taking a moment to recognize it is motivational. It lets them know how their good work is making a difference and encourages more of the same. If Maybin had followed her initial reaction, the conversation would have taken a totally different turn, and she would have missed out on that valuable feedback.

Active listening is the key to unlocking management's ability to benefit from employees' collective experience and points of view. Expressing genuine interest and curiosity in what they're saying is the ultimate form of respect, and one of the best ways of improving a workplace relationship, provided the listener's attention span remains uninterrupted.

It's also important to exercise self-regulation, as Maybin did, when confronted with information we believe is factually wrong, unrealistic, or offensive. While it can be frightening to listen without judgment when we hear criticism, shutting the speaker down before letting them finish destroys a learning opportunity and harms the relationship.

Managing Interruptions

I appreciate how easy it is for electronic distractions to disrupt active listening. We've become wired to respond to every beep and boop as if they're all of equal importance and require our immediate attention or the world comes to an end. They're not. They don't. And it won't. Sometimes it's spam.

Unfortunately, jumping whenever a new message arrives keeps us from being present and communicates to those we're listening to that they are less important than an electronic beep. It's disrespectful. No one appreciates having their conversation preempted by automated bells or whistles. Putting the interlopers on "hold" elevates the relationship in the room by giving employees undivided attention. It's one of the easiest ways to improve workplace connection.

Sure, there may be times when we need to be interrupted. Some events are time sensitive and really do require immediate attention. They simply can't wait. But letting someone know up front that the conversation may be cut short helps manage employee expectations, and scheduling time to complete the discussion later confirms it's importance.

--------(**FAIRNESS FACTOR**)--------
Fairness is about giving employees undivided attention during meetings and following up when communications get interrupted.

Actively listening takes practice. The respect it pays the speaker plus the sense of belonging it fosters makes it a skill well worth honing. Unfortunately, we can often be our own worst enemy in that effort because one of the biggest obstacles we face is our own listening preferences. It can hamper our ability to absorb valuable information because we may unknowingly tune out when the material is presented in a way that's at odds with our dominant listening preference.

Listening Preferences

Dr. Kittie Watson has identified four types of listening preferences. People-oriented listeners are generally interested in relationships. They respond best to examples and stories and tune out when the conversation is not focused on them or the speaker's language is not inclusive. Action-oriented listeners like to get to the heart of the matter quickly, preferring information in outline form. Content-oriented listeners want as much information as possible and like to delve into the nitty gritty of statistics and data. Time-oriented listeners focus on schedule, efficiency, and effectiveness, and feel disrespected if their time is wasted with poor preparation or tardiness.

Each listening style has strengths and weaknesses, and in looking over Dr. Watson's categories, some may resonate more strongly with us than others. That's fine. As managers, it's important to identify how our own preferences, especially our most dominant preference, can cause us to miss learning opportunities so that we can adjust and allow all employees to feel heard and understood.

FAIRNESS FACTOR

Fairness is about listening with compassion and curiosity
to learn and understand other points of view.

According to Dr. Watson, organizations who really listen to their employees are twelve times more likely to retain them as compared to those who don't. That's why listening and being curious are so important and why her firm, Innolect, has developed assessments designed to measure and track our ability to listen.

Unfortunately, too many people in power believe they have all the answers, or need to have all the answers, when in fact their real power comes from knowing what questions to ask, listening, and inviting participation. It requires a growth mindset.

Gratitude and Growth Mindset

Expressing gratitude and demonstrating a willingness to listen without judgement for the purpose of learning encourages employee collaboration. These skills empower employees by engaging them in joint problem-solving. It inspires cohesion and sense of belonging because people support that which they help create.

Gratitude acknowledges how the decision-making process is enriched when everyone's voice is heard. It fosters teamwork. Even more, the prestige associated with sharing opinions also confers esteem on the contributors and checks off a motivational box on Maslow's Hierarchy of Needs that strengthens the implied social contract. Best of all, it robustly demonstrates a growth mindset in action. It is the direct opposite of the know-it-all-ism and the arrogance often associated with the misuse of power in organizations.

─────(**FAIRNESS FACTOR**)─────
Fairness is about adopting a growth mindset
to actively encourage teamwork.

I believe I have a growth mindset but don't think my team necessarily sees it that way. What can I do to demonstrate it?

One way to is to borrow from the world of improvisation.

Whoa . . . improv? My business is no joke. Get serious!

I am serious, and I appreciate that improv sounds counterintuitive. But "the root of improvisation however isn't to entertain," according to business trainer and improv professional Milo Shapiro of PublicDynamics.com. "The idea behind it is to be able to think on one's feet, react quickly, and find good solutions to things when they come up. It requires good listening skills, building upon the ideas of others, non-verbal communication, and creative problem-solving." As a result, improvisation has much to offer business leadership.

One common improv technique that helps stimulate collaboration is the simple phrase "yes, and . . . ." Please note, the phrase is "yes, *and*"—not "yes, *but*." Rather than automatically discarding ideas, "yes, and" acknowledges the person's idea (not necessarily validating it) and opens the floor to brainstorming with the next person adding to the initial observation using the "yes, and" format.

Sure, on the comedy stage the goal is laughs. When used in business it allows ideas to stumble forward. Each iteration moves the team closer to a successful resolution. Even when there's a concern, saying "yes, *and* we need ideas for solving [the issue] or "thanks for bringing that up, and we might consider handling [the issue] by doing [solution]." The technique helps advance the conversation while recognizing the earlier contribution and opening the door to the next avenue of exploration and collaboration.

Expressing appreciation for the willingness of workers to share their knowledge and point of view shows the organization values their talent. It shows they matter. It encourages cooperation by keeping information and ideas flowing. The process not only inspires productivity and innovation, it also helps surface problems while they are small and less costly to address. It's a great way for leaders to obtain employee buy-in and move the business forward.

The Difficult One-on-One Conversation

Yeah, it all makes sense. But what if I need to have a difficult conversation with an employee? How can I do that with all these niceties, this empathy stuff? I might have to tell someone the cold, hard truth.

Ah, yes. Allow me to introduce you to Darrin.

Most employees don't get called to their immediate supervisor's office without knowing what it's about. That's why when it happens, it's not without a touch of trepidation. Will it be good news or bad? Darrin, a project manager on a manufacturing company sales team, was no exception.

The vice president I had the privilege of working with at the time discovered Darrin's performance and behavior wasn't up to par. Others on the team noticed it too and voiced their displeasure about picking up Darrin's slack. After consulting with me about the legal landscape regarding involuntary separation, he scheduled a meeting with Darrin. Now, it was showtime.

Many executives would focus solely on the errant behavior, cite company policy and the cold, hard facts, and then start walking the employee up the disciplinary ladder with the top prize being the fall from grace and an escort out the door. But this vice president took a different approach. He instead discussed the performance and behavior at issue in a factual, non-judgmental way, asking what Darrin thought was happening. Believing that it wasn't due to incompetence, but of something else, the vice president wanted to learn what "it" was.

Sure enough, after a short discussion his "tell me more" approach led Darrin to confide his heart was no longer in the job. It wasn't a good fit. The dialogue continued with Darrin sharing his career aspirations and the vice president agreeing to help him transition to another department or employer.

Darrin left the meeting relieved. He had an ally in moving forward. The team was grateful their message had been heard and that the additional workload and stress they were experiencing would be short lived. Similarly, the vice president was pleased a legal headache had been side stepped.

The executive's attention to relationship building with his team is what earned him the trust needed to resolve the problem with Darrin. He got to know them and their work. He was a sounding board for their frustrations and provided guidance when they felt overwhelmed or were uncertain about how to do something. Being heard and understood created the psychological safety they needed to speak freely with him about Darrin's performance, and for Darrin to speak honestly about what his real issue was. It's hard to be without empathy once you get to know someone.

This executive paid attention and respectfully listened to his team without judgement or distraction. He also exercised self-regulation and compassion to find a mutually beneficial solution for Darrin. Together, these approaches demonstrated good faith and left everyone feeling better to one degree or another.

Contrary to what some may believe, leaders don't need to be afraid of losing control or being taken advantage of by their employees when being attentive to their feelings. It is possible to have difficult conversations that demonstrate good faith and fair dealing and simultaneously advance the best interests of the organization, as the deft handling of Darrin's situation illustrates. It does not need to be an either/or, zero-sum, proposition.

(FAIRNESS FACTOR)

Fairness is about allowing trusting relationships
and a growth mindset to inform win-win solutions.

The Nexus of Self-Awareness and Relationship Chemistry

Healthy workplace connections and self-awareness of individual relationship chemistry don't develop on their own. They require being alert to how our behavior impacts others. Attentiveness helps us identify and resolve problems before trust is irrevocably lost.

Imagine for a moment if Darrin had been working in a fear-based culture. Concern about being dismissed on the spot, or otherwise retaliated against, would have kept him from being honest with his supervisor. The problems Darrin had been creating for the team would have continued, dragging everyone down, forcing the executive's hand and creating a potential legal headache.

Fortunately, the vice president's self-awareness and skill in communicating with empathy created the climate of trust and safety needed to solve Darrin's situation quickly *and* successfully, contributing to his reputation for fairness and accountability. It made his team a sought-after assignment, attracting the best talent in the building.

The positive, feel-good energy that allows people to trust and be comfortable enough to open up is usually attributed to a leader's personality. But according to the brain and behavioral research conducted by Daniel Goleman, trusting relationships are really forged by exhibiting more self-awareness, impulse control, and empathy.

Calibrating Our Communication Chemistry

The power of effective communication and its role in supporting high-performance cultures can't be overstated. Ironically, "many managers really do believe they're being as honest and transparent as they can be, and the illusion that such communication has successfully taken place can be attributed to their lack of self-awareness," says Duke's Professor Sim Sitkin.

Since successful leaders generate trust and goodwill with their employees by demonstrating empathy, it's helpful to break it down into simpler components that are easier to discern. It's a task Figure 5.1, the Table of Key Relationship Elements, is designed to support.

When evaluating our ability to connect with others, we need to ask ourselves how many interactions, or communication elements, reflect the left-hand side of Figure 5.1 versus the right-hand side. Do our verbal and nonverbal messages, when combined and evaluated as a whole, largely reflect understanding or indifference? Do they promote trust or fear? The more anxiety and trepidation management creates, the more those activities contribute to the norms nobody wants to talk about.

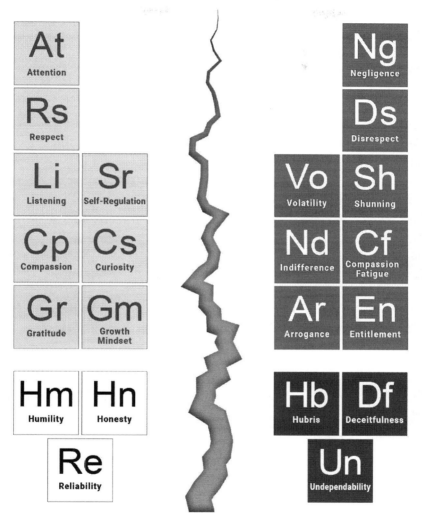

Figure 5.1 Table of Key Relationship Elements

There are countless ways to combine these elements to create a signature style that lets employees know they're understood and valued; but given management's positional power, it doesn't take much negative energy in the form of hubris, deceitfulness, or undependability (the three character traits grouped at the bottom of the right-hand side of Figure 5.1) to overshadow the positive elements and infuse the organization's culture with fear.

When employees become fearful, they get more guarded and reserved in the name of self-preservation. It transforms the social contract relationship equation. Employees wanting x+ but only getting x from employers will recalibrate and next time match management's x with y amount of employee engagement. Fear sparks dissatisfaction and short-circuits the pluses of full engagement.

Little things really do mean a lot says Anne Baum, author of *Small Mistakes, Big Consequences: Develop Your Soft Skills to Help You Succeed*. Employees, especially new hires who are learning to navigate the organization's cultures, are always assessing the strength of their connections with their supervisor to determine whether management can be trusted. That's why the more humility, honesty, and reliability leaders display, the greater the reservoir of trust and goodwill they can build and draw on when inevitable slipups occur.

FAIRNESS FACTOR

Fairness is what strengthens workplace relationships,
infusing them with trust and goodwill.

We're only human. Nobody is perfect; there are bound to be some elements from both sides of the divide in Figure 5.1 present in our interactions from time to time. It's the quality and quantity of the elements that determine the degree of trust between the parties, employees' commitment to the job, and amount of discretionary effort they bring to work. Assessing how individual managers communicate provides valuable information that can be used to customize a professional development plan to strengthen those skills for the purpose of improving workplace relationships.

OK, alright already, I get it. But what does all this have to do with those norms you were talking about earlier?

Communications are nuanced and so is the awareness needed to address the different types of norms nobody wants to talk about. In

Chapter 4 we analyzed the importance of internal awareness (our own values and beliefs), external awareness (how we present ourselves), and social awareness (how we're perceived by others). We also paired the five most common norms nobody wants to talk about with the mindfulness needed to help remedy each situation in Figure 4.1. But awareness alone fixes nothing. I might, for example, be aware that my car's fuel gauge is nearing empty, but that alone doesn't fill the tank. I need to take action.

Addressing the behaviors that sink employee engagement and retention numbers requires action too. Communicating with empathy is essential. But what kind of empathy? That's what Figure 5.2 on the next page illustrates. It adds to the existing framework our newfound understanding of communication chemistry by showing how it can bring positive energy into the room, and can contribute to trusting workplace relationships.

Each row of Figure 5.2 is a mini road map for how greater awareness can unlock the empathy needed to understand the employees' perspective. These communication techniques can improve perceptions of empathy and fairness that strengthen workplace relationships. Research from MIT's Human Dynamics Laboratory found that a team's communication patterns were its most important predictor for success, confirming that what we say and how we say it matters tremendously.

Although leaders don't need to be perfect, when management behaviors contradict the stated values of the organization, when they their actions fail to reflect the covenants of good faith and fair dealing, and especially when they do so with impunity and without accountability, the organization is really saying is *the rules don't matter and certain people can say and do whatever they want*. That's why improving communication skills is important, as are systems of genuine accountability to encourage more empathy and self-awareness, since those are the guard rails necessary to keep the organization's culture on a healthy track.

	Self-Awareness	Relationships
Unapproachability		
Unavailability Ignoring/Shunning Lack of Empathy	How We Present Ourselves	Curiosity Listening Growth Mindset
Lack of Recognition		
Wage Theft Timely Compensation Subjective Rewards Credit Stealing No Feedback	How We're Perceived	Respect Gratitude Compassion
Bias		
Microaggressions Bullying Discrimination Harassment	Our Internal Values and Beliefs	Attention Respect Self-Regulation Compassion
Poor Conflict Management		
Volatility Conflict Avoidance Gaslighting Retaliation	How We Present Ourselves	Attention Respect Self-Regulation Compassion
Poor Workload Management		
Unclear Communications Micromanaging Unrealistic Goals Lack of Support	How We're Perceived	Curiosity Listening Growth Mindset Attention Respect

Figure 5.2 How Empathy Can Address the Norms Nobody Wants to Talk About

Before diving into the next chapter on accountability, let's recap the fairness factors related to relationship building that influence perceptions of good faith and fair dealing and what they teach us about improving employee engagement, retention, and satisfaction:

- ✓ Fairness is about reconciling communication style and tone to improve connection.

- ✓ Fairness in remote electronic conferencing and written communications is about striving for clarity and compensating for missing verbal and visual cues.

- ✓ Fairness about keeping workplace communications professional.

- ✓ Fairness is about choosing and using communication channels wisely.

- ✓ Fairness is about emotional self-regulation.

- ✓ Fairness is about making time to actively listen and learn without judgement.

- ✓ Fairness is about giving employees undivided attention during meetings and following up if communications get interrupted.

- ✓ Fairness is about listening with compassion and curiosity to learn and understand other points of view.

- ✓ Fairness is about adopting a growth mindset to actively encourage teamwork.

- ✓ Fairness is about allowing trusting relationships and a growth mindset to inform win-win solutions.

- ✓ Fairness is what strengthens workplace relationships, infusing them with trust and goodwill.

Chapter 6

Make Genuine Accountability a Cornerstone

A ccountability is typically associated with liability and punishment. Something bad happens and someone must be held responsible. Calls to lawyers start with, "I have an employee problem," and end with, "Can I fire them?" When management exasperation reaches a boiling point, accountability becomes a nuclear option.

Hey, you got a problem with that?

I appreciate there are times when employee separation is necessary and appropriate, but using accountability exclusively to part ways misses out on the huge advantage it can give leaders to build great teams.

Advantage? What do you mean by that?

In its broadest sense, accountability is about responsibility. It's not merely obsessing over why the proverbial glass is half empty and expectations haven't been met. It includes evaluating the half full part: whether the proper foundation for performance has been laid, whether expectations have been fully communicated and understood. In the employment context, accountability means looking at whether employees are doing their jobs *and* whether management is giving them the support needed to fulfill their duties and obligations, as previously discussed in Chapter 1 and reprised in Figure 6.1.

THE SOCIAL CONTRACT

Figure 6.1 Mutual Responsibilities

In implied social contract terms, it's literally about the rules of engagement: both parties' reasonable expectations and mutual understandings. In other words, did employees get what they needed so they could give management what they wanted? Has there been good faith and fair dealing? It's a two-way street.

(FAIRNESS FACTOR)

Fairness is about remembering accountability
is a two-way street of good faith and fair dealing.

Given the need for good asset stewardship and the imbalance of power between supervisors and their direct reports, getting more mileage from the accountability process puts the onus on leaders to reflect with self-awareness on how much reasonable support they have given their employees before pulling the trigger and disciplining them.

The questions managers need to ask themselves are: Do employees really understand what's expected of them? Have they been given the proper information and reasonable resources needed to complete their mission? If so, how? And when? If not, what's missing? And why?

(FAIRNESS FACTOR)

Fairness is about reflecting on whether employees have been
given reasonable support before disciplining them.

Reasonable support means carrying out the implied social contract with employees in good faith and with fair dealing. As we've seen in Chapter 2, falling short creates workplace norms nobody wants to talk about. Those unproductive patterns are largely due to the inherent nature of power itself (Chapter 3), a lack of self-awareness (Chapter 4), and suboptimal communication skills (Chapter 5). While those factors explain how and why employee-employer relationships get strained and broken, they don't excuse it. The implied social contract is still breached. Accountability, however, is an excellent method for keeping employee engagement and retention on track by creating guardrails to protect the relationship from undercurrents that would otherwise undermine it.

The Power of Accountability

Accountability speaks to what the company really stands for—its values and honesty. It's a litmus test of allegiance to those principles and evidence of whether fairness still exists in the $y+ = x+$ equation. When used to enforce acceptable conduct, accountability incentivizes good citizenship in organizations and demonstrates how what employees do and how they do it matter. When the management focus is on maintaining standards of good faith and fair dealing, it supports a culture of belonging and joint problem-solving. When accountability is arbitrary and based on ad hoc decision-making, it spawns norms nobody wants to talk about.

{ FAIRNESS FACTOR }

Fairness is about using accountability to incentivize and empower a unifying code of conduct based on good faith and with fair dealing.

It can be challenging to manage worker expectations fairly throughout the employee relationship deal life cycle (making, tending, mending, and ending, see Figure 6.2 next page). Having a better understanding of when and how hiccups happen during these stages gives managers more control over accountability, enabling them to proactively manage misplaced expectations that threaten the implied employee-employer social contract.

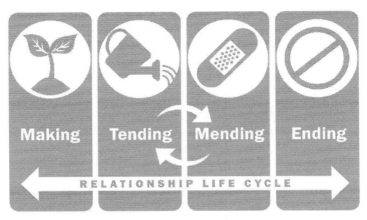

Figure 6.2 Employment Relationship Deal Life Cycle

FAIRNESS FACTOR

Fairness is about using accountability throughout
the employment relationship as a system for
managing the parties' reasonable expectations.

Fairness in the Dealmaking Process

We're all familiar with the deal*making* phase of the relationship life
cycle. The recruiting and hiring processes are supposed to help us avoid
ugly surprises. Ideally, they clarify mutual expectations by screening
up front for competence and cultural compatibility. In reality each side
looks to make a great impression while a peek behind the curtain tells a
slightly different story.

It reveals an eager job applicant looking for a payday and new
opportunity, and an equally eager organization wanting a qualified warm
body to fill a necessary role. In the need for speed, it's not uncommon for
organizations to gloss over the unsexy parts of the job and for applicants
to tell interviewers what they want to hear. It's not that either side
seriously intends to mislead the other. It's merely a timing issue. They
just haven't gotten around to telling each other everything yet. They
also hope once they get to know each other better, their idiosyncrasies
will be forgiven and goodwill maintained.

One survey found 25% of employees believed they didn't get enough information about their job before accepting the offer, and only 40% said their current job was accurately described during the interview process. That left a whopping 60% who thought their job description was inaccurately represented. These new hires discovered the truth during the onboarding process and the first few months on the job, and when they realized their day-to-day role wasn't what they expected, 64% of them quit. Their perception of a massive broken promise led them to completely *disengage.*

Not every job disappointment or broken promise merits such an extreme reaction. Most people are more proportional in their response. Nonetheless, it doesn't mean perceived breaches of the social contract don't produce some degree of disengagement and employee blowback, or that repeated violations don't have a cumulative effect that ultimately causes a minor incident to break the proverbial camel's back.

Isn't that a bit melodramatic? No organization is pristine, and it's not like they're lying when they skip over, say, the boring aspects of a job during the interview process.

True. It might not be a lie; but it is misdirection. If the information being glossed over or omitted is material to the job applicant's ability to make an informed decision about a job offer, it will ultimately lead to less employee satisfaction, engagement, and retention.

───────┤ **FAIRNESS FACTOR** ├───────

Fairness is about full disclosure in job descriptions to manage an applicant's expectations and enable their informed decisions.

Ironically, what one person thinks is boring bureaucratic detail may be intriguing to another. The applicant's skill set and perspective matter more than those of management because it's the new hire who will be doing the job. Allowing an employee's talents to shine by properly aligning their interests and strengths with the job's real requirements leads them to have a more satisfying employment experience. When someone enjoys their work and they're good at it, they'll be more engaged, not to mention more productive and innovative.

It simply doesn't pay to fudge the facts. Doing so is an example of unclear communications that contribute to poor workload management and detracts from employee satisfaction. Yet, with some forethought it's easy to remedy.

Fairness in the Deal Tending Process

The deal tending phase of the implied social contract is where performance under the agreement takes place. It puts everyone's expectations and trust to the test. It's where both parties are presumed to keep their end of the bargain in the $y+ = x+$ equation, where employees are expected to deliver full engagement ($y+$) in exchange for a satisfying employee experience that includes a sense of belonging (collectively $x+$). The benchmarks for those expectations, as discussed in Chapter 1, are the covenants of good faith and fair dealing in the implied employee-employer social contract. It requires honest compensation and working conditions and management not acting contrary to the spirit of the agreement.

Employee performance is dependent on management's support: reasonable deadlines and deliverables, timely information, feedback, and resources. The ability to provide such assistance requires management's self-awareness. It's about being curious without being overbearing or micromanaging and listening for the purpose of understanding what employees need to be successful in their jobs. It can also include coaching and mentoring to empower resilience and inspire appropriate risk taking without fear of retaliation, plus encouragement by recognizing a job well done. Altogether, it's about respecting employees' need for safety and belonging to do their best work.

Of course, staying informed about employee progress and performance requires open and honest communications. No one is a mind reader. That's why constructive dialogue is critically important. It makes explicit our respective implicit expectations. Of course, *how* those messages are conveyed ultimately determines whether such communications empower or disenfranchise higher performance. Do those conversations generate positive energy? Or negative? It's a management choice that's pivotal in meeting the covenants of good faith and fair dealing, as well as employees' human motivational need for safety, belonging, and esteem, as summarized in Figure 6.3.

FAIRNESS FACTOR

Fairness is about open and honest communications that empower mutual understanding and inspire higher achievement.

	Self-Awareness	Relationships	Accountability
Unapproachability			
Unavailability Ignoring/Shunning Lack of Empathy	How We Present Ourselves	Curiosity Listening Growth Mindset	Deal Tending
Lack of Recognition			
Wage Theft Timely Compensation Subjective Rewards Credit Stealing No Feedback	How We're Perceived	Respect Gratitude Compassion	Deal Tending
Bias			
Microaggressions Bullying Discrimination Harassment	Our Internal Values and Beliefs	Attention Respect Self-Regulation Compassion	Deal Tending Deal Mending
Poor Conflict Management			
Volatility Conflict Avoidance Gaslighting Retaliation	How We Present Ourselves	Attention Respect Self-Regulation Compassion	Deal Mending
Poor Workload Management			
Unclear Communications Micromanaging Unrealistic Goals Lack of Support	How We're Perceived	Curiosity Listen Growth Mindset Attention Respect	Deal Making Deal Tending

Figure 6.3 How the Energy People Bring into the Room Impacts the Implied Social Contract and the Human Motivational Needs of Maslow's Hierarchy

Unfortunately, too many managers are uncomfortable giving negative feedback. They avoid it altogether or sandwich it between two positive pieces of information—which means it doesn't get heard. They would rather revise a forecast or edit a report themselves instead of sending it back with comments or instructions for how to fix errors and make improvements. Avoidance may sidestep awkward conversations and create the illusion of saving time, but it adds to management's workload.

When the pattern repeats itself, it also creates a pressure cooker of resentment that eventually explodes with "You're fired," leaving the unsuspecting employee wondering what they did wrong. How were they supposed to know if nobody told them?

Providing feedback is a learning opportunity for employees. Communicating the good, the bad, and the ugly with empathy helps them discover how to do their jobs better. It can also document an employees' progress and growth, or lack thereof, to help make the case for raises, promotions, or if necessary, deal ending.

"Deal tending is an ongoing performance review
focused on supporting higher achievement."

Too often the request for corrective action gets lost in translation. Research by Professors Schaerer and Swaab shows managers often unintentionally sugar coat criticism due to the "illusion of transparency." It's a common cognitive bias that causes the speakers to overestimate the degree to which their own internal feelings or intentions are conveyed by vague language.

Take for example the catchphrase characterizing something as "a real possibility." Of course, the word *possible* doesn't necessarily mean "probable," yet Schaerer and Swaab found people interpreted the expression to mean "likely" 20%–80% of the time. That's a huge difference in understanding and a wide margin for disappointment. It demonstrates the importance of clarity, honesty, and accuracy in our communications.

───────(**FAIRNESS FACTOR**)───────
Fairness is about communicating with clarity, honesty, and accuracy.

Well, I understand the importance of honest communications, but what if the problem is them, not me? Some people mix like oil and water. We have personality conflicts. What good does any of this self-awareness stuff do when talking to them feels like walking on eggshells?

Personality conflict is how we label and write off a "difficult" person. We treat it as an issue beyond our control and outside our scope of management responsibility. Yet, we're really crossing swords due to incompatible communication styles. It results from a mutual lack of social awareness. Since management is part of the problem and in a position of power, they also need to be part of the solution.

Self-awareness, or mindfulness, is actually a huge asset for resolving perceptions of personality conflict. Research shows internal awareness of our own conduct makes us inclined to see our behavior as a reaction to what others do. If, for example, we're rude to someone whom we feel deserves it, we don't believe it makes us a terrible person. We see the event as a one-off occurrence, a response to being provoked. We may view our external behavior as a way of asserting ourselves, setting the record straight, and restoring healthy boundaries. A necessity.

When we assess other's personality, research finds we're more apt to think in absolute terms. We're less contextually forgiving. We're likely to believe others are boorish individuals rather than ill-mannered in a single moment because we're socially unaware that we might have provoked *them*.

FAIRNESS FACTOR

Fairness is appreciating that "personality conflicts" are really incompatible communication styles requiring more mindfulness to solve.

Ideally both the employee and their immediate supervisor would commit to developing more social awareness by focusing on how their respective styles impact each other and members of their team. After all, the implied employee-employer social contract is a two-way street. And some supervisors *do* have successful discussions about how to improve team interactions.

During a training session I conducted when one employee was upset about being cut off mid-sentence during meetings, it was agreed they could use their hand to signal the other person to stop. It worked. Eventually the interruptions ended; sadly, such candid discussions and fixes don't happen as often as they should. Instead, too many people simply dive into the emotional deep end and point blame. Opinions calcify. Trust evaporates, and workplace relationships tank.

Timing is critical. That's why deal tending matters. Management often waits too long to acknowledge their role in a communications chicken-egg dance and then jumps to conclusions about someone else's personality or intentions instead. When this happens, their internal perceptions harden, leaving little room for negotiation, compromise, or trust. It's not a fun way to work. It can manifest in external behaviors of exclusion that further derail a sense of belonging and hamstring trust. It's a common cause of team dysfunction.

To break this vicious cycle management needs to remember that someone else's behavior is as variable and situational as their own. Individual messaging styles are layered and subject to multiple interpretations. With more self-awareness, management can identify ways to clarify their message and improve their workplace relationships during the deal tending stage of the employment life cycle.

-------(FAIRNESS FACTOR)-------

Fairness is about using power and influence
to anticipate and mitigate misunderstandings.

Four out of the five most common workplace norms nobody wants to talk about from Chapter 2 can be remedied with better deal tending as illustrated in Figure 6.4 next page.

Paying attention to how employees are communicating with management, being curious about whether they believe they have enough access, and adopting a growth mindset to improve availability can sidestep approachability issues before they become unproductive fixtures of organizational culture.

Indeed, asking employees, "How can I support you?" or "Is there anything else you need from me?" can open up an interesting dialogue. Even if their answer is, "I'm good" or "I have what I need," just knowing management is standing by and willing to help provides a safety net that encourages inclusion and promotes a sense of belonging.

	Self-Awareness	Relationships	Accountability
Unapproachability			
Unavailability Ignoring/Shunning Lack of Empathy	How We Present Ourselves	Curiosity Listening Growth Mindset	Deal Tending
Lack of Recognition			
Wage Theft Timely Compensation Subjective Rewards Credit Stealing No Feedback	How We're Perceived	Respect Gratitude Compassion	Deal Tending
Bias			
Microaggressions Bullying Discrimination Harassment	Our Internal Values and Beliefs	Attention Respect Self-Regulation Compassion	Deal Tending Deal Mending
Poor Conflict Management			
Volatility Conflict Avoidance Gaslighting Retaliation	How We Present Ourselves	Attention Respect Self-Regulation Compassion	Deal Mending
Poor Workload Management			
Unclear Communications Micromanaging Unrealistic Goals Lack of Support	How We're Perceived	Curiosity Listen Growth Mindset Attention Respect	Deal Making Deal Tending

Figure 6.4 How Accountability Can Address the Norms Nobody Wants to Talk About

FAIRNESS FACTOR

Fairness is about soliciting employee feedback
to demonstrate support and approachability.

Being more thoughtful about how appreciation for a job well done is doled out can address issues associated with a lack of recognition.

There's a huge difference between a heartfelt thank you and one said with clenched teeth or a pre-printed Employee Engagement of the Month Club thank-you note that's here today and gone tomorrow. Employees recognize when management's non-verbal behaviors don't align with their words. They can tell when supervisors are merely going through the motions.

Honest compensation, paid in accordance with applicable laws, is essential to fair recognition and good faith deal tending, especially when market conditions change during the course of the employment relationship. Wages that fail to keep up with inflation or technology advances that threaten the terms of employment and ability to make a living, such as artificial intelligence that endangers intellectual property rights such as a person's likeness, need to be addressed, not exploited. An organization that is unable or unwilling to honestly address such issues with employees on a one-to-one basis may not only find themselves enabling a culture of low employee engagement, they may also find themselves fending off union organization and employees finding a voice through the power of collective bargaining.

──────(**FAIRNESS FACTOR**)──────
Fairness is about genuine recognition that
keeps pace with changing market conditions and the law.

Deal tending is ideally an ongoing performance review, marked by constructive learning and joint problem-solving opportunities. Some organizations still rely heavily on annual year-end appraisals. While such assessments *should* never surprise employees, they're often seen by employees as having little to do with their performance or contribution to the company, and merely as thinly disguised mechanisms to justify a predetermined raise or deny a promotion.

Perceptions of subjective rewards are fueled by supervisors who base their reviews on what they remember an employee did last week or last month. Last-in first-out performance appraisals are only surpassed by my personal favorite: The Pearl Harbor File. It's when a reviewer packages all their grievances into a cluster bomb and drops it on the unsuspecting worker in an annual performance review. What's sad about this tactic is how instead of dealing with issues as they arise in real time, when circumstances can be explained and behaviors modified, they're compounded through continued avoidance, making the situation worse for all involved. Either approach to performance reviews undermines management's duty of fair dealing. Some would even call such actions passive-aggressive or deceitful.

Oh, come on, it's really hard to give negative feedback to someone, especially if they're a high performer. We need them and don't want to antagonize them.

No one ever said leadership is easy. It is possible to sharpen conflict management skills to address problematic behavior. Paying attention to our own internal values and beliefs while giving criticism or advice and engaging in self-regulation can help steer clear of biases that contribute to microaggressions, bullying, discrimination, and harassment. Yet sometimes, despite management's best efforts, a conflict can't be avoided.

FAIRNESS FACTOR

Fairness is about having the courage to conduct
difficult conversations with compassion.

Fairness in the Deal Mending Process

Life isn't perfect. People on both sides of the desk can make mistakes or be misunderstood. It creates a conflict continuum of issues large and small that require deal *mending*, the process whereby the relationship speed bumps are smoothed over, and deal tending equilibrium is restored.

It's not a matter of *if* the employee-employer relationship hits a rocky patch, it's only a matter of *when*, and whether management can successfully get things back on track and chugging along. It happens. When leaders tell me they have no problems on their teams, it usually means they're not looking hard enough. Glitches are what managers are here to solve, and *how* they do it is what separates the great ones from the rest.

I can handle problems with my employees, and I know when they're wrong and I'm right!

I'm sure you do! The belief of people in power that they are more right than anyone else is not uncommon and one of the leadership blinders discussed in Chapter 3. Unless we're talking about something clearly illegal, the name of the game in deal mending and conflict resolution is to identify the facts, the underlying interests, and ways to compromise. There are as many ways to look at a situation as there are people involved, and reaching an agreement does not necessarily mean splitting the difference. Sometimes that's not even possible. Imagine a hostage negotiator telling a kidnapper, "I'll take the blonde; you keep the brunette."

Asking "What's fair?" was one of my favorite questions in a negotiation workshop I used to teach. We'd explore the concept by negotiating the settlement of a family estate, the type of conflict that commonly leads to bitter disputes and estrangement among family members.

The case study I used had each of the adult siblings inheriting an equal share of the estate. Cash generated by the sale of property was easy to split, but there were five items the heirs agreed not to sell: a family vacation cottage, an oil painting, an heirloom silver dinner service, some antique furniture, and the contents of the family library including rare books. Each item had a different market value, not to mention sentimental value, and each sibling had a favorite one . . . or two. There was no simple way to equally divide the goods. The math didn't work.

What was remarkable to me about the exercise was how unique each team's solution was given the small number of facts. Results were never identical no matter how often I ran the simulation. Similar, yes. Identical, no. The combinations and permutations were as varied as the participants. It made me realize that no matter how simple or straightforward the facts may appear, a fresh set of eyes will always bring a new perspective. There was no "right" answer, and active listening enabled creative compromises that led to amicable solutions the group determined was fair.

One team, for example, had a particularly imaginative answer for the vacation cottage. They combined individual ownership with vacation timeshare rights for the rest of the siblings to give them all an opportunity to create special memories with their children. Another team handled the silver dinner service by giving one family member "custody" with the understanding that the others could borrow it for special occasions and hosting family holiday gatherings. It assured the heirloom pieces would continue to play a continuing role in family traditions.

By focusing on underlying interests instead of doubling down on who can force their will upon others, they were able to achieve mutual satisfaction. They were curious and asked questions to learn more about *why* a certain item mattered, and *how* it mattered. They engaged in learning conversations. It helped surface powerful information about intangibles an antiseptic spreadsheet could never capture, transforming those interests into deal sweeteners that bridged gaps and helped them reach consensus. The process of respecting the relationship by acknowledging competing interests and finding common ground led them to fairness.

Solid conflict management skills are an essential part of a business leader's repertoire and pivotal to maintaining healthy workplace relationships and high-functioning teams. When done well, it provides an opportunity to improve mutual understanding, strengthen workplace bonds, and increase trust. If done poorly, or not at all, it contributes to the norms nobody wants to talk about. And this is exactly why accountability is so valuable and why the self-awareness we analyzed in Chapter 4 and self-regulation discussed in Chapter 5 are essential to optimize its functionality. The sooner managers recognize they have a problem the sooner they can engage in constructive conversations to preserve, and potentially increase, employee satisfaction, engagement, and retention.

FAIRNESS FACTOR

Fairness is about protecting the employee-employer relationship
by communicating in good faith to identify interests
and negotiate mutually acceptable solutions.

Sometimes workplace conflicts are difficult to address. It makes me uncomfortable when employees come into my office riled up and start having emotional meltdowns.

I agree. It can be scary when someone storms in with a problem or sits down and starts crying. We might not initially know whether the source of their frustration is us or something else. Either way, their negative energy feels threatening, easily triggering our own emotional response. As managers we need to control the urge to react to someone's strong feelings with our own. Our goals instead are to identify the underlying ignition source and get the blaze under control.

Unfortunately, research finds that anger reduces our ability to see things from other people's perspective. That's why self-regulation and empathy are essential to conflict resolution. Dropping the hammer by using positional power can shut down unpleasant conversations. But, without addressing the problem's root cause, the frustrations can bubble up in another form of accountability, such as litigation, whistleblowing, or even violence. Low employee engagement or retention may be the least of organization's worries in those situations.

OK, so what am I supposed to do? I can't just sit there.

Rather than view an employee's anger as a personal attack, it's useful to note people get upset when expectations go unmet or promises are broken. They depended on something that was important to them and were deeply disappointed when it didn't happen. The lack of reliability it represents violates their trust, and their anger is a means of expressing how much they care about the breach and the relationship behind it. Redirecting that energy into a positive learning and joint problem-solving conversation is the key to smart conflict resolution and keeping employee engagement alive.

---------(**FAIRNESS FACTOR**)---------

Fairness is about channeling conflict into a
positive learning and joint problem-solving dialogue.

It can be a challenge to find out what happened or what expectations have been trounced when an upset employee shares a stream of consciousness. Dr. Debra Dupree, a dispute resolution specialist and conflict leadership coach, offers a two-part communication strategy she uses in mediations to reduce the temperature and transform strident ramblings into constructive dialogues.

During our podcast interview she advised it's necessary to redirect the brain out of its emotional part into the cognitive part. Start with a helpful phrase such as, "I can see that you're really upset." The acknowledgement is then followed up with "What I'd like to suggest is that you go ahead and take five minutes to sit here by yourself, and I want you to write down three or four, maybe even five key things about what happened, so we have something to focus on when I come back, and we can come up with a plan of action and move forward."

Dupree's simple two-part conversation starter accomplishes a number of things: (1) it recognizes the employee's feelings without passing judgment, (2) it communicates the employee has been seen and heard, (3) it creates a cooling off period to disengage the amygdala, (4) it lets the employee present their perspective of what happened and why it matters in writing, (5) the document gives managers a concrete starting point to understand what happened and ask follow-up questions, (6) it reassures the employee of developing an action plan, (7) it offers hope of an equitable resolution, and (8) it moves beyond feelings toward actions that can accomplish something.

Recognizing that connections with colleagues and direct reports are fluid and knowing when to toss a life preserver instead of casting stones can make all the difference in the world to the employment experience. Good conflict resolution skills promote psychological safety and are a leadership superpower.

--------(FAIRNESS FACTOR)--------
Fairness is about protecting psychological safety.

But sometimes the only way to resolve an irreconcilable workplace conflict is to part ways.

Fairness in the Deal Ending Process

While it may be emotionally satisfying in the moment to blurt out a Donald Trump-style "You're, fired" and demand security accompany the errant employee out the door in a corporate perp walk, public humiliation is rarely a smart tactic.

Former employees can often be a valuable source of new hire referrals or future business opportunities. If they leave angry about the terms of their departure, those prospects evaporate—poof! Their subsequent fury could also reignite anger over workplace betrayals they had previously let slide, visiting legal liability on the company or individual managers, in retaliation for being let go. One study that examined litigation patterns of terminated employees found that workers who felt they were treated unfairly by their former employer during the termination process were twenty times more likely to sue than those who thought they were treated fairly.

Even worse, aggrieved former employees could commit workplace violence as happened in the 2019 shooting at the Henry Pratt Company plant in Aurora, Illinois, where an employee left five people dead after opening fire inside the warehouse after having been fired. Of course, no one expects it to happen to *them*. But neither did they.

It takes an engaged effort on management's part to understand what employees are experiencing says workplace violence prevention expert Felix Nater. "There are many, many reasons why an employee may come to work preoccupied with issues that may affect his or her workplace or workplace relationships," he says. Taking an aggressive posture is not productive. "The primary objective should be to ask many questions that help you arrive at a solution that is amenable to the workplace retention, . . . the resolution of problems, or even an eye-opening opportunity to help the employee through his or her particular issues."

Nonetheless, sometimes separation is inevitable. It can occur for a number of reasons: better career opportunity, need to relocate due to a partner's job change, full-time return to school, military deployment, retirement, change in family circumstances, death, or even winning the lottery. Regardless of why an employment relationship ends, fairness demands the separation be honored with dignity and respect to reasonably minimize collateral damage. It's the civilized thing to do.

─────────┤ FAIRNESS FACTOR ├─────────

Fairness is about mutual respect during the employment separation process to reasonably minimize collateral damage.

If the scope of accountability has been fairly communicated and managed throughout the employment life cycle, the likelihood of separation becomes less of a surprise and the emotional heat surrounding separation more subdued and anticlimactic. Employees who see the inevitable writing on the wall have an opportunity to look for another job and continue meeting their basic needs. Similarly, employers receiving notice can ramp up their recruiting process to minimize disruption to essential business functions.

Business is about relationships: creating them, maintaining them, fixing them, and accepting irreconcilable differences with grace. And the real power of accountability stems from the cultural safety net supporting it.

Before diving into the next chapter on the cultural safety net, let's recap the fairness factors related to genuine accountability that influence perceptions of good faith and fair dealing and what they teach us about improving employee engagement, retention, and satisfaction:

- ✓ Fairness is about remembering accountability is a two-way street of good faith and fair dealing.

- ✓ Fairness is about reflecting on whether employees have been given reasonable support before disciplining them.

- ✓ Fairness is about using accountability to incentivize and empower a unifying code of conduct based on good faith and with fair dealing.

- ✓ Fairness is about using accountability throughout the employment relationship as a system for managing the parties' reasonable expectations.

- ✓ Fairness is about full disclosure in job descriptions to manage an applicant's expectations and enable their informed decisions.

✓ Fairness is about open and honest communications that empower mutual understanding and inspire higher achievement.

✓ Fairness is about communicating with clarity, honesty, and accuracy.

✓ Fairness is appreciating that "personality conflicts" are really incompatible communication styles requiring more mindfulness to solve.

✓ Fairness is about using power and influence to anticipate and mitigate misunderstandings.

✓ Fairness is about soliciting employee feedback to demonstrate support and approachability.

✓ Fairness is about genuine recognition that keeps pace with changing market conditions and the law.

✓ Fairness is about having the courage to conduct difficult conversations with compassion.

✓ Fairness is about protecting the employee-employer relationship by communicating in good faith to identify interests and negotiate mutually acceptable solutions.

✓ Fairness is about channeling conflict into a positive learning and joint problem-solving dialogue.

✓ Fairness is about protecting psychological safety.

✓ Fairness is about demonstrating mutual respect during the employment separation process to reasonably minimize collateral damage.

Chapter 7

Maintain a Cultural Safety Net

Effective talent management is a cultural safety net. It protects the implied social contract and the workforce's sense of belonging and safety in three powerful ways: (1) the hiring processes that screen for organizational fit, (2) the onboarding processes that welcome new hires into the company, and (3) the continuous professional development processes that facilitate personal growth aligned with the company's values and strategic goals. Each process component of the cultural safety net provides a unique opportunity to manage employee expectations and fulfill the covenants of good faith and fair dealing.

(**FAIRNESS FACTOR**)

Fairness is about using the hiring, onboarding,
and professional development processes to protect,
promote, and strengthen the company's culture.

The recruiting and hiring process plays a key role in protecting the existing workforce's good faith expectations of physical and psychological safety by screening candidates for technical and behavioral compatibility. We all know that the skillset and mindset of new hires matters. Yet too often new people are brought into the organization in an ad hoc fashion. Interview questions are improvised. The candidate pool is limited to a friend, or a friend of a friend, who needs a job; and offers are extended based on a gut feel or sense of camaraderie rather than objective criteria.

Such casual standards are problematic because they eventually bring people into the fold who breed the norms nobody wants to talk about. And sadly, the blinders justifying the unfortunate hiring decisions turn into validating excuses keeping the misfits on the payroll. The result: overall employee engagement, satisfaction, and retention suffers.

FAIRNESS FACTOR

Fairness is about using the hiring process to protect
the physical and psychological safety of the organization.

The onboarding process contributes to the cultural safety net by helping new hires learn about the company's internal stakeholders, policies, and procedures as well as the firm's history and external competitive environment. It's a short-term process of assimilation that promotes a sense of belonging and demonstrates fair dealing by providing valuable information to accelerate the new recruits' ability to be successful in their new role.

FAIRNESS FACTOR

Fairness is about using the onboarding process to
enable the productivity and success of new hires.

Personal and professional development is similar to onboarding; unlike the short-term orientation process, it adds the long-term view to the cultural safety net by seeking to expand workplace skills and proficiencies that facilitate organizational growth and effectiveness. The acquisition of new competencies benefits engagement by boosting employee confidence and supporting their psychological need for esteem. Investing in training and professional growth also increases employees' ability to deliver higher performance. It's a win-win. But tapping those benefits requires a mindset shift of recognizing human capital as an asset capable of appreciating over time instead of a disposable transaction cost.

─────(**FAIRNESS FACTOR**)─────
Fairness is about treating employees as valuable assets
instead of disposable transaction costs.

When viewed as a whole, hiring, onboarding, and continuous education, as illustrated in Figure 7.1, support the cultural integrity and sustainable growth of the organization. Strengthening the safety net can therefore be a smart way of using talent management to improve employee engagement, retention, and satisfaction.

Figure 7.1 The Cultural Safety Net

Improving Hiring Processes

Hiring is part of the deal making process we previously examined in the context of accountability. Where accurate job descriptions zero in on the candidate's technical competencies, the cultural safety net focuses on behavioral competencies: their people skills.

A piece of paper can only reveal so much, regardless of whether it's an application form, a resume, or a curriculum vitae. A friend of mine learned that lesson the hard way after bringing a post-doctoral candidate on to her university research team based solely on their fabulous credentials. Once he reported for duty, she quickly discovered his eye-watering personal hygiene habits made collaborating in the confines of a small science laboratory too challenging.

Meeting in person after an initial screening gives decision makers more information to evaluate a candidate's cultural fit. It's an opportunity to assess the energy they bring into the room, their communication style, their self-awareness, how they think and problem solve, and their approach to power. It's an essential step, especially when filling management positions where it's helpful to know their inclinations before entrusting them with the organization's precious human capital. It's important to know whether they can steer clear of the five most common employee engagement killers—the norms nobody wants to talk about: unapproachability, lack of recognition, bias, poor conflict management, and poor workload management.

It's easy to make assumptions about someone based on first impressions, how we get along with them, and especially by how much they remind us of ourselves. But recruiting is the first line of defense in "keeping the enemies at the gate" says HR Culture Czar Jim Jeffers, founder of HRrenewal®.

We want to trust our gut instinct, yet given what's at stake it's important to have a system in place to compensate for our blind spots. The goal is to find the person best suited to help the company get where it wants to go, not find a golfing buddy. We need people who are trustworthy corporate citizens, who will respect organizational values, and who support a healthy workplace environment, not those who merely pay lip service to it in an interview.

I know what you mean. We've had people slip through who in hindsight we wish hadn't. But some folks are just incredibly persuasive and good at interviewing. What can we do to keep from being misled?

It's a common dilemma and a great question. No one wants to be conned into hiring someone who is ultimately a suboptimal fit for their business. And yes, there's plenty we can do to protect the organization.

Creating Structure and Standardization

Developing an interview guide for the position being recruited provides structure and standardization that contributes to more informed decision-making according to Kathleen Quinn Votaw, CEO of

TalenTrust, a strategic recruiting and human capital consulting firm. It's really important to know the position's key technical competencies, the target behaviors required to be successful in the job, and especially the questions we need to ask to probe for them she says.

FAIRNESS FACTOR

Fairness is about creating and maintaining
a structured and standardized interview process.

Interviewing is stressful for all involved. Job candidates are as anxious about making a good impression as we are in having them confide in us about their work experiences and foibles. Achieving that comfort level requires building rapport. Some introductory pleasantries and an easygoing conversational style transitioning into open-ended questions (that are not prohibited by law) is one way to help put candidates at ease.

But devising open-ended questions can be daunting. When asked about it, Andrea Hoffer, founder, and CEO of AHA Recruiting Experts, suggested beginning with the power phrase "could you share a specific example" or "specific time" to preface a scenario related to the job as an effective way to keep the conversation relaxed and get candidates to open up about their experiences without it sounding like a Klieg light interrogation.

To illustrate further, Hoffer said if one of the requirements for the job is taking initiative and ownership of things, an interviewer might phrase the question as, "Could you share a specific example of a time at work where it wasn't clear who was responsible for a certain task?" Presenting the situation and not leading the candidate by saying, "How did you solve it" can be illuminating. Did they think it was their issue to solve? Did they take charge? Or were they waiting to be told what to do?

The Power of Probing Questions

Probing questions reveal who job applicants *really are*, not who they say they are on paper or online. It can indirectly disclose problem-solving capabilities in ways that rehearsed answers to standard questions such as, "What are your greatest strengths or weaknesses" never will.

Topics to formulate questions around include what's the best job they ever had and to explain why. Or conversely, the worst job they had and why. Then listen carefully to discover what tipped the scales in favor or against certain circumstances. Was it the tasks involved? The person they reported to? Or the environment as a whole? What excited them? Bored them? Why are they looking to change jobs? What motivates them? The answers can be enlightening about their leadership acumen, workload management (taking responsibility for getting the job done), conflict management (sidestepping or defusing landmines), and recognition (giving it or needing it).

Ask about their typical workday. How do they handle interruptions? Conflict? How do they make difficult decisions? Present them with a recent business situation that would be within the scope of their responsibilities if they came aboard, and ask how they'd handle it. Such questions reveal real-time problem-solving skills and creativity.

Will their solution reflect cultural competencies? Will they present a plan to seek more information and express a desire to get buy-in from stakeholders, or will they already "know it all?" The answers can tell us a lot about their perceptions of power and influence. Do they lean autocratic? Or collaborative? Are they consistent? Or is one style used when managing up the chain of command and another down? And don't forget to debrief colleagues who are also conducting interviews to allow the next person to follow up on vague answers or other concerns. Careful listening and smart follow-up questions allow conversations to build on one another.

When Actions Speak Louder Than Words

How candidates treat office personnel during onsite visits can also offer insight into their beliefs about authority, empathy, and bias. One hiring manager, for example, liked to pose as the office receptionist, welcoming candidates as they entered the lobby and evaluating how they acted toward someone perceived to be lower on the totem pole than the position they were applying for. Some were courteous, and those who weren't were later chagrined to find her conducting their interview in the conference room.

Business lunches or dinners are another time-honored acid test of privilege and civility. Will they be polite? Or hard to please? Will they even see the waitstaff as people? Or merely as "the help?"

Broadcast journalist and political commentator Anderson Cooper, tells a fascinating story how one summer, as a young man, he worked as a waiter at a society restaurant in New York City called Mortimers. He had eaten there many times with his mother, fashion designer and heiress Gloria Vanderbilt, and her friends. Yet when he served those same people in his waitstaff role, they didn't recognize him and treated him very, very differently than when seated next to his famous mother. The experience had a profound effect on him.

Being self-aware of our internal values, how we present ourselves, and how we're perceived, as explored in Chapter 4, is a linchpin to more effective and productive workplace relationships. Probing for it is one of the things HR Culture Czar Jim Jeffers deems vitally important. "A lot of toxic people really manage up well and interview well," he says. That's why toward the end of a meeting he likes to ask, "Okay, this has been a great discussion, but if you could go back and change anything in this interview, what would you change?" For Jeffers it's a test of self-awareness and honesty because in his experience toxic employees have a "woeful lack of self-awareness." They never do anything wrong.

Short Cut Risks

These are all great points, but they feel like a big hassle. I don't have a lot of time, and we hire infrequently. Why can't I simply hire someone and see how it works out? What's the big deal?

Hmmm, interesting question. The big deal is that to the outside world your employees are the company, and legally they are your agents when acting within the scope of their duties. It means their behaviors, both their acts and omissions, are attributable to the organization even if their immediate supervisor has no direct knowledge of it. Sure, it could mean scoring a profitable sale. But it could also spell trouble. It's a sobering thought.

Whether rolling the dice on cultural, financial, or reputation loss is ultimately a big deal depends on management's risk tolerance. How upset will the board of directors or investors be if an errant hire creates a scandal or public relations nightmare? How distraught will the existing workforce be?

Impulsive hiring decisions jeopardize employee trust and confidence in management. The harm bad hires inflict on a business culture reverberates long after the misfit leaves according to Dr. Mitchell Kusy, author of *Why I Don't Work Here Anymore*. It's antithetical to safeguarding existing employee engagement, satisfaction, and retention.

Business social climbers who have polished their interviewing skills are masters of obscuring their dark side. It takes an average of two years for companies to admit they have a problem employee and then actively do something about them. Imaging how much damage could be done in the meantime, how it can injure company culture, hurt external relationships, tarnish reputations, and trigger lawsuits or regulatory inquiries.

I can tell you from my own experience that cutting corners in the hiring process can be an expensive mistake. In one case, when an internal audit revealed someone in the finance department had misappropriated funds, further investigation found the person had a previous fraud conviction. It was a big oopsie that could have easily been caught in a thorough background check. But did they do a background check? Hmmmm, no.

FAIRNESS FACTOR

Fairness is about exercising due diligence in the hiring process.

Preemployment Assessments and Background Checks

"People are the number one weakest link in business," says Candice Tal, licensed private investigator and CEO of Infotel Worldwide. That's why robust interviewing and background investigations, along with appropriate preemployment assessments, offer an additional margin of safety in the hiring process. Those background checks are most effective when layered and based on individual job requirements, the amount of sensitive data they'll have access to, and the degree of fiduciary responsibility they will have says Tal. Typical reviews include verification of educational, employment, and criminal history, as well as social security and address confirmation, and sometimes credit history.

Yeah, I've seen links to online sites offering individual background investigations you can do yourself. For a nominal fee, databases even provide criminal histories. And of course, you can learn a ton from someone's social media postings.

Yes, I've seen those online links, too. But a word of caution. Tal says many of those advertised databases are extremely limited. It's not uncommon for them to mismatch names, causing false negatives and positives, especially if the candidate's name is common. They also fail to identify half of all criminal convictions, and often omit international searches and portions of the web not indexed by search engines. Those vast hidden pockets are often called the deep, dark, or historical web and require special browsers, encryption keys, or paywall subscriptions. They're bigger than the Google, Yahoo, or Bing searches we typically associate with the Internet.

In one investigation Tal noted a U.S. background check came back squeaky clean, but an international search turned up a red flag for possible money laundering. A deeper dive into the person's country of origin found issues ranging from bribery, corruption, and racketeering, to murder. An inexpensive database search would have missed that information. That's why it's important to verify the reliability of the resources we depend on in making hiring decisions.

──────(**FAIRNESS FACTOR**)──────

Fairness is about using reliable background
screening tools in the hiring process.

As for social media, it's not uncommon for companies to believe they can poke around because it's all public and free. Another word of caution is in order. Please speak to an employment lawyer before diving in. It really is possible to get too much information about someone. Finding out through Instagram, TikTok, Facebook, YouTube, or whatever that the person under consideration is in a protected class, has a hidden disability, or is undergoing fertility treatments, for example, and then using that data to influence a negative hiring decision has the potential of landing an employer in legal hot water.

To avoid claims of illegal discrimination it's important the tools used to conduct these inquiries are implemented in a legal and equitable fashion. Any preemployment screening, whether an aptitude test, a drug test, or background investigation should always be reasonably tailored to the specific responsibilities of the position being recruited for and fully compliant with all applicable laws. Foresight is definitely significantly cheaper than hindsight in these matters. That's why consulting with an employment attorney before plunging into the deep end is a smart investment of time and money.

FAIRNESS FACTOR

Fairness is about utilizing employee assessments and background investigations in an unbiased and equitable manner, in full compliance with all applicable laws and regulations.

Well, so many of these issues you've talked about here, like fraud, sound like big business problems. Mid-size and smaller companies can probably skip those detailed background checks.

I once thought so, too. Then I met Kelly Paxton. She's a certified fraud examiner, author of *Embezzlement: How to Detect, Prevent, and Investigate Pink Collar Crime*, and a former special agent with U.S. Customs whose idea of bad guys was the stereotypes we see on television. As a fraud examiner she learned we also need to look out for "nice guys."

During our interview Paxton explained how the rate of fraud in smaller organizations is double that of larger companies because bigger organizations have internal and external auditors who discover irregularities sooner. When fraud takes longer to find, the financial losses tend to be bigger. In her experience, the linchpin to fraud in smaller organizations is a trusted lower to mid-level employee who knows where every penny is, has access to the money, and isn't subject to procedural checks or balances.

The Special Challenge of Recruiting Management

The nature of the job and level of responsibility should always inform decisions about background investigations, especially at the senior levels. In Tal's experience, about 20% of the executives they screen have serious no-hire issues ranging from fake academic degrees to phony social security numbers that in one case hid a seven-year prison record for manslaughter while on cocaine, along with other drug convictions.

Concealed aliases Tal says have unearthed situations involving money laundering, bribery, racketeering, bankruptcies, undisclosed business ownership and board involvement that posed conflicts of interest, Securities and Exchange Commission violations, sexual harassment, and intellectual property theft. If such information were to become public after a manager was hired, it could be problematic. It could spell serious financial and reputational loss for firms in the for-profit sector and erosion of the donor base in the nonprofit arena.

It is precisely because recruiting is the first line of defense in "keeping the enemies at the gate," as Jim Jeffers says, that fairness demands the process stay focused on the best interests of the organization. Objective background investigations are powerful tools that supplement impressions and information gleaned in face-to-face meetings. They help answer the important question of whether the applicant under consideration is likely to enable the destructive workplace norms nobody wants to talk about, see Figure 7.2 next page.

FAIRNESS FACTOR

Fairness is about protecting the best interests of the organization by using the hiring process to "keep the enemies at the gate."

Improving Onboarding Processes

The onboarding process is the first real taste a new recruit has of the company. It's a prime-time relationship-building opportunity, one that shapes the implied employee-employer social contract by putting a capital B in *belonging* and demonstrating fair dealing by providing access to information and tools needed to be successful on the job.

	Self-Awareness	Relationships	Accountability	Cultural Safety Net
Unapproachability				
Unavailability Ignoring/Shunning Lack of Empathy	How We Present Ourselves	Curiosity Listening Growth Mindset	Deal Tending	Hiring Process On-Boarding Development
Lack of Recognition				
Wage Theft Timely Compensation Subjective Rewards Credit Stealing No Feedback	How We're Perceived	Respect Gratitude Compassion	Deal Tending	Hiring Process On-Boarding Development
Bias				
Microaggressions Bullying Discrimination Harassment	Our Internal Values and Beliefs	Attention Respect Self-Regulation Compassion	Deal Tending Deal Mending	Hiring Process On-Boarding Development
Poor Conflict Management				
Volatility Conflict Avoidance Gaslighting Retaliation	How We Present Ourselves	Attention Respect Self-Regulation Compassion	Deal Mending	Hiring Process On-Boarding Development
Poor Workload Management				
Unclear Communications Micromanaging Unrealistic Goals Lack of Support	How We're Perceived	Curiosity Listen Growth Mindset Attention Respect	Deal Making Deal Tending	Hiring Process On-Boarding Development

Figure 7.2 How the Cultural Safety Net Can Address the Norms Nobody Wants to Talk About

All too often employee orientation, as it's also known, is viewed as a mere administrative function of getting people signed up for payroll and benefits, showing them their workspace, introducing them to a few of their colleagues, and giving them a policy manual. If they're lucky, someone will take them to lunch the first day. After that, they're on their own.

The first days and weeks at a new job tend to be unsettling. It's simply the nature of the beast, and finding ways to smooth the transition with a more organized and comprehensive process can pay huge dividends that benefits everyone when it comes to employee engagement, satisfaction, and retention.

Research by BambooHR finds organizations with structured onboarding report 54% greater new hire productivity. Their research also indicates 89% of the employees who have experienced effective onboarding say they feel very engaged in their work, and 91% feel a strong connection to their organization. Further research by Click Boarding, an onboarding software company, found companies with a structured onboarding process experienced 50% greater new hire retention rate.

Think back for a moment on your own experiences in the early days at a new job. We're learning who's who and what's what and wanting to make a good first impression with everyone we meet. What events or milestones helped you feel welcomed and solidified a sense of belonging? When you had all the equipment and password access needed to do your job? Remembered coworkers' names? Received your first paycheck and were officially "in the system?" When you knew who to go for help? Were able to exercise decision making authority without being second guessed? Being recognized for your contributions? What did it take?

And how long did it take? A week? A month? Longer? The answers to those questions can help inform the structure of a successful onboarding process.

Structuring Onboarding

Feeling welcomed and accepted is a fundamental part of an employee-employer relationship that starts in earnest immediately after a job offer is accepted. The interval between acceptance and the employee's start date is pivotal because the new hire could still be receiving offers from other organizations. That's why it's the ideal time for sending a welcome letter or an email that includes materials to help them get better acquainted with their new employer.

Including recent company news, an annual report and information on company leadership, a summary of employee benefits, and a Frequently Asked Questions sheet to help answer common concerns assists in building greater new hire connection according to Barbara Mitchell and Cornelia Gamlem, co-authors of *The Big Book of HR*. Enrollment forms and a list of items to bring on the first day of work to complete the I-9 form in the U.S. are also useful. Bonus points go to sending a package that includes available company swag, whether a pen, t-shirt, or a mug because they're visible way of communicating, "Welcome to the team."

FAIRNESS FACTOR

Fairness is about building a solid employee-employer relationship immediately after the job offer is accepted.

The opportunity to reinforce a good first impression and create a sense of belonging also carries over to the new hire's first day at work. Letting existing staff know a new team member is arriving, facilitating access with the necessary parking permits and security authorizations for building entry and network permissions, making sure a new hire has a clean, functional, and appropriately equipped workstation, as well as identifying who to contact if they need help are all ways of saying, "Welcome—we've been expecting you."

When those basic things are missing, it's akin to checking into a hotel only to find our reservation misplaced and our room not yet ready. It's not a great start to an extended stay. Just as getting our bearings when visiting a new place bolsters our independence, confidence, and ability to get around, a new employee orientation program serves the same function.

A well-structured curriculum manages new hire expectations about institutional values, culture, history, and personnel. It introduces important policies and facilitates the employee's learning curve regarding compliance. Videos and other forms of technology can help make policies and other information come to life and assure consistent messaging for the company.

Avoiding Overwhelm

Of course, the challenge of any employee orientation program is to avoid overwhelming someone on the first day or first week on the job. After all, the process is called onboarding, not waterboarding. Drowning people with paperwork and information only serves to frustrate and confuse them. Giving them equipment or tools they may not know how to use is another source of frustration. It can contribute to unnecessary tech-shaming and age bias that cuts both ways across generational divides. Older employees may be learning new apps, cloud storage and screencasting software while younger workers may be discovering the idiosyncrasies of copy machines and telephone landlines.

When new tech savvy interns in an office environment for the first time needed to print paperwork, they assumed the copier's touchscreen would make it easy. When they tapped "print" and nothing happened, they first confirmed the machine was plugged into a working wall outlet. When they pressed "print" again and nothing happened, they next checked the ink and toner. When printing still eluded them, they finally discovered the copier was out of paper.

Not all equipment or software is created equally, and not everyone's experience in working with them is the same. Helping new hires successfully navigate such gaps with short demonstrations or instructions makes it easier for them to be productive.

A best practice in onboarding, according to Mitchell and Gamlem, is to set realistic goals and 30-, 60-, and 90-day check-ins with new hires to answer questions and concerns. Spacing out the follow-ups allows latent issues to surface and earlier missed issues to be addressed.

---------- (**FAIRNESS FACTOR**) ----------

Fairness is about pacing the employee onboarding experience and
not overwhelming new hires with information and technology.

Including Relationship Expectations to Build Trust

The institutional components of onboarding, the policies and so forth, are vitally important because they establish cultural guardrails and boundaries. However, the relationship component of onboarding is the secret sauce that rarely gets the attention it deserves.

Performance under the implied employee-employer social contract is driven by behaviors influencing trust. These behaviors determine the speed of employee engagement and productivity, either accelerating it or slowing it down with the workplace norms nobody wants to talk about.

That's why smart supervisors have early meetings with new hires to discuss their preferences for progress reports, their availability for questions, the types of issues requiring management's prior approval, and how to raise thorny problems. Such conversations help manage expectations and mitigate the norms nobody wants to talk about regarding unapproachability, poor workload management, and conflict management (see Figure 7.2).

FAIRNESS FACTOR

Fairness is about managing expectations regarding communication styles and decision-making authority during the onboarding process.

Such discussions can be powerful because as described in earlier chapters, how we communicate and how self-aware we are play important roles in building trust and enabling employee engagement, satisfaction, and retention. That's why identifying communication preferences early in the employee-employer relationship can go a long way toward avoiding frustration and misunderstanding on both sides of the desk. But in practice, instead of directly spelling them out, such basic operating procedures get assumed instead.

People bring with them communication customs from past jobs, or for the younger cohorts, the patterns established with peers at school and in online spaces. What we say and how we say it matters and can significantly impact workplace relationships.

The use of unfamiliar business jargon, for example, is a source of confusion among Gen Z, with 57% claiming they waste time several times a month to figure out their meaning. The biggest offending phrases reported in the United States, for example, are "ducks in a row," "out of pocket," "too many cooks in the kitchen," "drinking the Kool-Aid," and "circle back." Yet Gen Z have their own communication habits that leave older workers scratching their heads to decipher the significance of emojis and punctuation or phrases that have been ascribed new meanings. Establishing some simple ground rules early helps keep misunderstandings to a minimum, especially when communicating with third parties and in formal business settings.

Using Communication Channels

Our electronic devices and apps continue to put more means of communication at our fingertips than ever before. However, the productivity these tools enable can be both a blessing and a curse. Which is the best to use? And when?

A public relations firm experienced that dilemma when it used multiple messaging apps to communicate internally. Confusion and bruised feelings occurred when employees missed an important meeting because it was announced on one platform and not the other. Knowing which app was primary and required closer monitoring could have avoided that mishap. It's but one example of why clarifying expectations about communication channels matters.

If someone leaves a voice message, do they expect a phone call in return? Or a text message? How quickly is a reply expected in either case? What's an acceptable window of time? And what response rate is expected while traveling for business, on vacation, on weekends, or during other non-business hours? What negative inferences or conclusions will be drawn if the answer is "late?" What constitutes "late," and what happens if they are? How much trouble will someone be in?

These are important questions, and it's not just about employees knowing what's expected of *them*. It also about employees knowing what to expect of their *managers and colleagues*. What's the best time of day to reach their supervisor? Are impromptu drop-ins welcome? Or do they have gatekeepers who manage appointments? Far. In. Advance. How available are managers and colleagues to provide the information and resources employees need? How accessible? And when?

These often-unspoken rules about communication preferences are best made visible before conflicts arise. Answering these questions helps avoid anxiety and second-guessing by new hires and eases their entry into the company culture. Revisiting them with existing team members from time to time is another valuable way to address changing needs and safeguard consistency and transparency, especially around holidays when more workers are taking time off to be with families. Is there a backup plan in case there's an emergency?

Fairness is about making unspoken rules about communication
preferences visible before conflict arises.

The Myth of Hitting the Ground Running

*Hey, when I hire people with experience, especially managers and senior
executives, I expect them to hit the ground running. That's what we're
paying for. We don't have time to waste with all this handholding and twenty
questions.*

I appreciate how hiring someone for big bucks comes with big
expectations. That's fair.

What's unfair is expecting a top performer at one company
to immediately perform at the same level in a totally different
environment. Sure, they can initially get some things done. However, a
deeper appreciation of organizational dynamics is what equips them to
utilize their expertise and experience more strategically and effectively.
It takes time to assimilate into a new organization's culture and to learn
the hierarchy, language, decision-making structures, unspoken rules,
and especially any relationship challenges accompanying them.

The phrase "hit the ground running" is often attributed to a military
context where troops deployed by air or fast-moving vehicles need to
move quickly to avoid injury or capture. Yet those troops were prepared
with intelligence briefings before reaching their drop zone. Your
managers deserve the same courtesy through onboarding.

────────[FAIRNESS FACTOR]────────
Fairness is about not assuming prior career success is a substitute for
onboarding and the time needed to process organizational dynamics.

Management-level onboarding may look different than for other
positions in the company. There may be nuances to services and product
lines, geographies, customers, legal constraints, and competitive
environments that take time to fully comprehend and should not be
skipped. Treating it like an episode of the TV show *Survivor* unnecessarily
sets up senior hires to fail. Indeed, according to a report by McKinsey,

up to half of new CEOs fail within the first 18 months, and more than 90% wish their transition had been managed differently. Investing time to help these leaders succeed is time well spent on the investment made in hiring them and in supporting the organization's culture.

Improving Personal and Professional Development

Personal and professional development is highly prized by today's workforce and a valuable component of the cultural safety net contributing to greater employee engagement and retention. One survey, for example, finds 92% of employees think professional development is important or very important. It also notes that those who have access to such training are 15% more engaged and have a 34% higher retention rate.

But what exactly does personal and professional development mean? What do employees want?

I'll tell you want employees want. They want my job. They want promotions. But we can't make our organization top heavy, so there's no real point talking about it. The job's the job. They can take it or leave it.

Ah, but what if you knew promotions weren't upper most in the minds of employees when thinking of career development? What if there were a more granular way to look at the subject that could simultaneously boost employee engagement and productivity?

I'm listening.

It turns out that promotions ranked dead last in a survey of over 10,000 working professionals, regardless of age, gender, rank within the hierarchy, or geographic location in the U.S. based on a study done by Julie Winkle Giulioni, a champion for workplace growth and development, and author of *Promotions Are SO Yesterday*.

Here's what mattered more to the group: (1) contribution, the ability to make a difference aligned with their strengths and values; (2) competence, increasing critical skills and expertise; (3) confidence, trusting and appreciating their talents; (4) connection, building and enhancing their workplace relationships; (5) challenge, stretching beyond their comfort zone to make a difference; (6) contentment, experiencing satisfaction and joy in their work; and (7) choice, enhancing the amount of control and autonomy they can exercise in doing their work.

FAIRNESS FACTOR

Fairness is about recognizing that professional
development encompasses more than promotions.

In essence, employee development is about enabling employees to perform their best work. It involves providing reasonable support and not acting contrary to the spirit of the implied employee-employer social contract agreement.

When employees know more and can do more it fuels their sense of confidence, accomplishment, and satisfaction, dovetailing with the human psychological need for esteem and belonging of Maslow's Hierarchy of Needs. Altogether it supports the covenant of fair dealing, as examined in previous chapters, and illustrated in Figure 7.3.

FAIR DEALING	Esteem	Belonging
Contribution	●	●
Competence	●	
Confidence	●	
Connection	●	●
Challenge	●	●
Contentment	●	●
Choice	●	●

Figure 7.3 Relationship Between Professional Development Preferences and Fair Dealing

Motivating Employees with Personal and Professional Development

Wait just a minute! In my experience a lot of employees, especially younger ones, simply don't want to work. They're not interested in doing more than necessary. So, I respectfully disagree with you about employees' innate desire of wanting to do "more."

I understand. It's an oft-heard sentiment. But I'd like you to meet Cheryl Johnson. She's an instructional designer and performance solutions specialist, as well as the author of *Ambition: The Missing Attribute in Your Employees.*

That's it! Ambition! That's what these people are missing. I bet she knows what I'm talking about.

When I interviewed Johnson to learn more about ambition and how it relates to employee engagement and productivity, she shared an interesting story with me about the time she was tasked with managing five college interns who frustrated everyone.

"These guys, they just come sit at work, put their headphones on, pull their hoodies over their head, and stare at the computer screen, and [they] don't get a whole lot done during the day," she said. They didn't ask many questions and didn't finish the projects they were assigned to either. They were clearly disengaged and underperforming.

[Groan!] She's seen my office. That's what I'm talking about!

In researching her book, Johnson learned there is a close correlation between confidence and ambition. Applying that discovery to the intern logjam, she decided to improve their confidence by managing their expectations in ways that allowed them to experience success, not more criticism. After all, who doesn't like success?

She did it by developing detailed policies and providing constant feedback. They were delighted to hear, for example, that they could work whatever hours they wanted, provided the work got done and didn't exceed 20 hours. However, they struggled with the idea of deadlines. They thought working whenever they wanted meant projects could be completed "whenever" too.

With constant coaching and mentoring Johnson was able to improve their work habits. Daily appointments to review assignments eventually became weekly meetings. They developed better time management skills, greater confidence, and a desire for more success, which translated into improved productivity. It took time, says Johnson. It was a process, and she glowingly reported that the intern who came to the table with the least amount of motivation became her biggest success story.

What I love about Johnson's story is how instead of criticizing the interns' disappointing performance and writing them off she inspired improvement by breaking down her expectations into bite-size pieces they could comprehend, digest, and achieve. She wisely recognized the root cause of the problem wasn't their innate capabilities. It was their lack of workplace experience and understanding of management expectations. They simply didn't know what they didn't know; and with better instructions, coaching, and mentoring they learned how to become more productive.

If we look at the professional development preferences identified by Julie Winkle Giulioni's research, as summarized in Figure 7.3, we see that Johnson's approach helped the interns by presenting a challenge and increasing their competence, which in turn improved their confidence and allowed them to make a better contribution in the workplace. Detailed policies and feedback, not formal classroom training, buoyed their esteem and provided the resources needed to do their best work.

FAIRNESS FACTOR

Fairness is about facilitating education to support employee esteem and belonging that enables more engagement and productivity.

Hey, I can't spend as much time with each of my employees as Johnson did with those interns. Besides, I'd be accused of micromanaging!

That's absolutely correct. The hiring process is where we want to be crystal clear about the job qualifications and experience needed for success and to weed candidates out accordingly. That doesn't mean even ideal employees won't disappoint on occasion and can benefit from some guidance to realign performance with company expectations. Similarly, before writing off employees, as many did with Johnson's interns, it pays to note that employee development needs are individualized and approaches to learning and training vary. There is a benefit to the organization in providing reasonable educational support. Indeed, it's a necessary part of fair dealing.

FAIRNESS FACTOR

Fairness is about appreciating that personal and professional development needs are individualized and approaches to learning and training are varied.

The Leadership Responsibility of Good Asset Stewardship

Good asset stewardship makes it incumbent on leaders whose expectations haven't been met to honestly ask themselves whether those expectations were explicitly communicated and really understood by employees. And if not, why not? Afterall, we can't fix a problem without knowing it's root cause, and since relationship issues are nuanced, getting to the heart of the problem may require asking "why" multiple times. Is it a communication issue? A competence issue? An intransigence issue? Or something else? Getting to the bottom of what's driving suboptimal performance is necessary to inform decisions about reasonable next steps.

FAIRNESS FACTOR

Fairness is about honestly identifying the root cause
of suboptimal performance to make more informed decisions
about reasonable professional development options.

Assuring Return on Investment

I appreciate the value of professional development to bring employee performance up to par. My concern is spending on education to enhance rather than remediate employee skills and then having the employee join a competitor or start their own business.

This is a reasonable fear, often based on a bad experience. It reminds me of companies that footed hefty tuition bills for high achievers to attend executive MBA programs and watched them take higher paying jobs elsewhere after graduation. They responded to the "problem" by limiting future candidates and adopting policies demanding tuition repayment prorated to their continued tenure after earning their degree. It was a punitive tactic that promoted an us-versus-them mindset and unnecessarily transformed tuition costs into a short-term transaction instead of a long-term investment to encourage learning and support a sense of belonging.

Well, la-di-dah! How am I supposed to protect the organization and a return on our tuition investment when it can walk out the door at any time?

Try giving them a reason to stay.

When we invest in remedial help for employees, we expect a return on training dollars in the form of improved performance. There is value on both sides of the desk. Employees get to keep their jobs, and the company gets better productivity.

But where is the *quid pro quo* when organizations invest in education designed to enrich and deepen an employee's competencies beyond their current job requirements? How are the employees incentivized to use their newfound knowledge in a way that benefits the organization? How can the learning be applied to optimize their role and create more job satisfaction?

---(**FAIRNESS FACTOR**)---

Fairness is about crafting personal and professional development opportunities that add value to both sides of the employee-employer relationship.

Brainstorming ideas with the employee about how to utilize their new skills *before* acquiring them facilitates thinking about how the organization gets a return on its investment and invites them to participate in conversations about optimizing their role. It helps manage expectations on both sides of the desk.

Will the new competency support better team results? Contribute to greater department or division productivity? Assist the organization with external stakeholders? Open the door to projects that present a challenge or assignments that afford more autonomy and choice and aide greater contribution? Giulioni says such discussions strengthen employees' sense of belonging by increasing the sense of meaning in their work. It reminds them of how they make a difference. It's incentivizing.

Retention of Hourly Workers

It sounds as if the personal and professional growth discussion is best suited for salaried workers who may be more invested in an organization as compared to hourly workers who may be more inclined to job hop.

That's an interesting observation and brings to mind a conversation I had with Scott Greenberg, author of *The Wealthy Franchisee*. The title of his book might at first lead us to believe franchise wealth is about building an empire of umpteen locations, but we'd be mistaken because his focus instead is on leadership strategies aimed at elevating team performance and unlocking the strength within.

Franchise businesses typically have high hourly employee turnover. The successful, or in Greenberg's vernacular the "wealthy," franchisees don't because in his words, "they look at [employees] as an opportunity and so they take time to really grow them as opposed to just direct their work." Facilitating that growth requires improving their skills through constructive feedback and recognition of what they're doing right.

Taking an active role in employee growth takes more than the occasional compliment. It requires thinking about the human aspects of work, appreciating that hourly workers have hopes and dreams, asking about their goals, and tapping into their values. It's about showing the organization cares about them as people. Franchisees who demonstrate such respect "experience a lot more retention, fewer headaches, and ultimately better customer service because they have motivated, talented employees who are engaged in their work and who really care," says Greenberg.

To illustrate, Greenberg shared a story about a franchisee for a window cleaning and Christmas lights franchise called Shine who gave him stock answers when asked about why they were so successful. But after some gentle prodding the franchise owner revealed he had a book club with all of his employees where he bought each of them a hard copy or audio version of a book they were interested in. They all read or listened to it, and then met to talk about it. He was the only franchisee in their system to do it, and it helped make his business the top performer. His was a creative and novel way of enabling personal growth and supporting a sense of belonging.

FAIRNESS FACTOR

Fairness is about recognizing hourly employees have
personal and professional growth needs, too.

The franchise story is a great example of how personal or professional growth can be woven into the organization's cultural safety net to support higher performance.

Let's recap of the fairness factors that influence perceptions of good faith and fair dealing in the cultural safety net and what they teach us about improving employee satisfaction, engagement, and retention:

✓ Fairness is about using the hiring, onboarding, and professional development processes to protect, promote, and strengthen the company's culture.

✓ Fairness is about using the hiring process to protect the physical and psychological safety of the organization.

✓ Fairness is about using the on-boarding process to enable the productivity and success of new hires.

✓ Fairness is about treating employees as valuable assets instead of disposable transaction costs.

✓ Fairness is about creating and maintaining a structured and standardized interview process.

✓ Fairness is about exercising due diligence in the hiring process.

✓ Fairness is about using reliable background screening tools in the hiring process.

✓ Fairness is about utilizing employee assessments and background investigations in an unbiased and equitable manner, in full compliance with all applicable laws and regulations.

✓ Fairness is about protecting the best interests of the organization by using the hiring process to "keep the enemies at the gate."

✓ Fairness is about building a solid employee-employer relationship immediately after the job offer is accepted.

✓ Fairness is about pacing the employee onboarding experience and not overwhelming new hires with information and technology.

✓ Fairness is about managing expectations regarding communication styles and decision-making authority during the onboarding process.

✓ Fairness is about making unspoken rules about communication preferences visible before conflict arises.

✓ Fairness is about not assuming prior career success is a substitute for onboarding and the time needed to process organizational dynamics.

✓ Fairness is about recognizing that professional development encompasses more than promotions.

✓ Fairness is about facilitating education to support employee esteem and belonging that enables more engagement and productivity.

✓ Fairness is about appreciating that personal and professional development needs are individualized and approaches to learning and training are varied.

✓ Fairness is about honestly identifying the root cause of suboptimal performance to make more informed decisions about reasonable professional development options.

✓ Fairness is about crafting personal and professional development opportunities that add value to both sides of the employee-employer relationship.

✓ Fairness is about recognizing hourly employees have personal and professional growth needs, too.

Chapter 8

Mend the Structural Safety Net

The structural safety net protects the organization's culture and supports its operational integrity. It's a roadmap for accountability and is often thought of as the policies establishing a code of conduct, a system for how work gets done. While those guidelines and procedures are certainly important items, they are only one piece of a bigger, supportive substructure.

No matter how well written or thorough policies and other governance documents may be, they are not self-executing or self-regulating. The expectations and responsibilities they outline require management's *commitment* to implement fairly and an appropriate incentive structure to encourage employee compliance, as illustrated in Figure 8.1 next page.

Sounds pretty straightforward and fair to me. What's the problem?

Consistent and reliable application of governance documents helps fuel employee trust and empowers more employee engagement. Mission statements talking about compliance with the law and treating employees with dignity and respect ring hollow when discrimination and other unfair behaviors are sheltered in leadership blind spots. Basic values get repudiated by the lack of empathy and awareness such power dynamics enable causing employee satisfaction, engagement, and retention to slip. That's the problem.

Figure 8.1 Overview of the Structural Safety Net

(FAIRNESS FACTOR)

Fairness is about consistent application of the organization's governance documents.

Governance Documents

Governance documents affirm organizational values. They are a special set of records, as illustrated in Figure 8.2 below, that capture the essence of company culture by identifying "*what* we do, *why* we do it, and *how* we do it."

Figure 8.2 Overview of Organizational Governance Documents

Governance documents, in a nutshell, consist of vision and mission statements; policies, programs, and procedures; and job descriptions. They are interdependent and build on one another, with each component giving employees a deeper understanding of how they're expected to contribute to the organization's success.

A vision statement, for example, identifies the company's purpose, it's direction and dreams for the *future*; the mission statement represents the *present* goals and objectives designed to enable the business vision; the policies, programs, and procedures constitute the *processes* needed for the smooth operational functioning of the organization to achieve its mission; and job descriptions offer a checklist of employee *experience and competencies* plus *responsibilities* each role needs to bring the mission and vision into fruition.

When viewed as a whole it's easy to see how they position the company for success by creating direction and safe guards to facilitate organizational growth and prosperity. Inspirational vision and mission statements are rarely problematic when it comes to fairness at work because they're aspirational. The more granular detail demanded of processes is where the hiccups can occur.

It should be noted that although articles of incorporation and other documents related to creating an entity can technically be considered governance documents, their focus is really on formation and the rights and duties of owners, not employees or workplace management practices *per se*. They are therefore omitted from our discussion.

Employee Handbooks

While job titles and descriptions may attract us to a particular employment opportunity and interviews acquaint us with an organization's vision and mission, it is the policies, programs, and procedures found in employee handbooks or manuals (collectively "Policies") that influence our day-to-day workplace experience.

Perceptions of unfairness surface when Policies aren't followed, when they're misaligned with the company's vision and mission, when there is a disconnect with the implied social contract's covenants of good faith and fair dealing, or when they run afoul of the law.

Wait a minute! Here we go with this implied contract thing again. When new hires join an established company, they're typically given a copy of the employee handbook during their orientation and sign a document acknowledging receipt and acceptance of its terms as a condition of employment. Isn't that a written contract between the employee and employer that overrides the fairness of the implied social contract you keep talking about? We set the terms and conditions in the handbook. They sign. Done deal. Right?

Yes, it can technically turn into a written contract if you're not careful and it's not as great as you might think.

Managers who believe a written employment agreement for rank-and-file employees is a good idea need to be cautious about what they wish for because that deal, at least in the U.S., can potentially transform an at-will employee into a contract employee. It doesn't simplify the relationship because the covenants of good faith and fair dealing exist in all agreements, regardless of whether they are written or implied. Instead, turning a policy manual into a formal written contract *limits* the terms of the agreement to the four corners of the employee handbook for both parties. And that can be problematic.

Problematic? How? Why? I thought having certainty is necessary to manage employee expectations. What am I missing?

Yes, a degree of certainty can be a good thing. It keeps *ad hoc* decisions from ricocheting like stray bullets through the organization. It can also be a straitjacket because it's impossible to include every conceivable situation in an employee handbook. Add too much detail that looks like an exhaustive list, and it invites workers to find a loophole and say, "You didn't tell me I couldn't do *that*, so it must be okay." Now the company is in a bind.

There may be times when a worker's conduct is so egregious that immediate separation is warranted; but, if the handbook rises to the level of a written contract that requires a verbal warning before a written warning and other progressive discipline before handing someone their walking papers, management is stuck. It can take a long time to discharge someone. Although contract employees can be relieved of their duties for cause before the end of a contract term, employee handbooks usually don't have defined end dates. As a result, a company could be locked into a toxic situation longer than it wants.

An at-will employee, however, can be relieved of their duties for any reason, or no reason at all. That's why best practices in the U.S. are for Policies *and* their acknowledgements to include a prominent disclaimer written in plain language that states workers remain at-will employees and no employment agreement is created by signing the acknowledgement, and that the handbook is to be used as non-binding guidance.

Keeping It Simple

Okay. So, if it's non-binding guidance, why do we need to be so formal? Why can't we keep Policies casual?

I understand how Policies make people's eyes glaze over. At large organizations such manuals can be tomes. When they exist solely online they can also be hard to navigate due to longwinded language and poor design layout making them difficult to read and understand.

Policies don't need to be written in clunky statutory language. "Very little is actually required by law, and yet, they're all written the same as if they were," says employment lawyer Rob Wood. "So, I think the first thing is to write in plain English in a way that they're really truly a tool for everybody in the business, including the owners."

I appreciate how early-stage businesses and entrepreneurs may bristle at the idea of formal Policies. When companies are small and especially when they're in startup mode, it's not uncommon for casual conversations to substitute for written Policies. Documentation feels bureaucratic especially when the quest for freedom and flexibility are what led business owners to start their own venture and be their own boss in the first place.

It's much easier to move the business forward when everyone understands the rules and knows where the foul lines are. As the number of employees on the payroll increases and business geographies expand, the need for consistency makes documentation imperative. It frees up the time it takes to tell new hires "everything" and assures everyone gets the same information in the same way. The uniformity also turns Policies into valuable reference tools.

FAIRNESS FACTOR

Fairness is about making sure all employees
understand the organization's rules.

"Employees can go there to understand the expectations, and the mangers can go there to know how to follow particular issues as they arise," says Wood. It eliminates guess work and misunderstandings, especially when the information is readily accessible and kept updated, whether online and/or in hard copy.

FAIRNESS FACTOR

Fairness is about making updated employee handbooks easily
accessible to consistently communicate the organization's vision,
mission, and key policies, programs, and procedures.

Policies don't need to be 500-page doorstops. To make them effective, they need to include the most important elements for the smooth functioning of the organization that encompass all stages of the employee life cycle (deal making, deal tending, deal mending, and deal ending—see Chapter 6).

Examples of reasonable topics to consider that also demonstrate good faith and fair dealing are identified in Figure 8.3. They may sound like common sense, but what constitutes common sense can dramatically differ among people based on their life experiences. That's why the best practice to avoid misunderstanding and conflict is to communicate essential standards and procedures in writing.

FAIRNESS FACTOR

Fairness is about adopting reasonable policies to create
a system for the smooth functioning of the organization
that demonstrates good faith and fair dealing.

	GOOD FAITH	FAIR DEALING
Code of Conduct, including for example: – Ethics – Conflicts of interest – Legal compliance – Dress code – Accountability	●	●
Employee programs, benefits, services, including for example: – Pay practices – Paid vacation, holidays, leave – Attendance & timeliness – Remote work	●	●
Workplace health & safety, including for example: – Accidents or injuries at work – Substance abuse – Workplace violence	●	●
Communications, including for example: – Cybersecurity – Acceptable computer, Internet, & email usage	●	●
Conflict resolution	●	●
Employee management, including for example: – Onboarding – Performance reviews – Offboarding	●	●
Jurisdiction specific requirements, including for example: – Equal employment and non-discrimination policies – Worker's compensation – Family medical leave	●	●

Figure 8.3 Sample Employee Handbook Topics

I've heard that there are software packages available that are "employee handbooks in a box." All the heavy lifting about what to include is already done. Wouldn't that be a simpler than starting from scratch?

Yes and no. While such off-the-shelf programs certainly help create a system, employment attorney Mimi Soule notes, "The details of the policies that might be embedded in those systems are typically one-size-fits-all, or way too complicated or convoluted for the typical business at issue." If maintaining flexibility is a management priority, "Then you wouldn't want to use any of the preloaded things that are in those systems; you would want to have them customized for you like any other type of software," she says.

Effective systems need to reflect how the company *actually* wants its managers to supervise their teams. It means the organization, not an app developer, should have the final say about company Policies. Otherwise, the proverbial tail wags the dog.

Great, now I feel like Goldilocks in the children's story with the three bears. How do I keep the Policies from being too hot, or too cold? What customization is needed to get it "just right?"

Excellent questions.

Policies should be instructional and getting it "just right" means having the correct content. Sounds simple, but it's easy to get distracted with alluring details in done-for-you packages that sound important but, as Soule notes, may be complex and ultimately meaningless because they don't apply to your company and are therefore impossible to adhere to. Extraneous information is the equivalent of being "too hot." It's clutter. It only confuses everyone.

On the flip side, prepackaged policies can be "too cold" when significant information is glossed over or omitted. Take for example generic pronouncements that end with language saying, "unless otherwise required by law," or words to that effect. Can that policy be taken at face value? Or not? The policy doesn't tell you. Instead, the language gives itself a get-out-of-jail-free card by shifting the burden of whether there's a local law limiting its effectiveness to the user. Without knowing what's authorized by the country or state where employees are located, it will be difficult to implement such policies correctly.

Knowing when additional laws might apply is critical, especially as more organizations embrace the competitive advantage remote work gives them in attracting the best talent anywhere in the world. Applicable local law is "one of the key things that's often missing in these handbooks," says Soule.

Overly restrictive language is another way one-size-fits-all employee handbook programs can leave management "cold." Take for example strict progressive disciplinary procedures that have no exceptions for circumstances when egregious employee behavior merits immediate separation. The inability to take action when appalling conduct tramples organizational values and/or threatens employee safety would be unfair to the remaining workforce, causing more problems than it solves, especially if faced with potential workplace violence. Adopting flexible Policies to ensure employee safety is therefore critically important.

FAIRNESS FACTOR

Fairness is about having policies and procedures that protect the physical and psychological safety of employees.

Ambiguous policy language can cause management headaches, too. Take for example the scenario where new hires are given 30, 60, or 90 days to prove themselves. When that timeframe is called a probationary period, it suggests permanent employment automatically starts the day after probation ends. That result may or may not be desirable. Describing it instead as an introductory or orientation period can afford management more flexibility by signaling additional approval is required before the position becomes permanent.

Policies that get it "just right" focus on the fundamental ground rules specific to the individual company, its size, its industry, and the jurisdiction in which it operates. Most of all they do so in a practical, non-controversial way. It's about zeroing in on the "key things that you need everybody to understand that works in your business and the specific procedures that you want them to follow, so that you're not getting gummed up and [you're] getting work done," says Soule. Organizations working in highly regulated fields, for example, will want to include information unique to their regulatory compliance needs. Large companies may need more detail than those with a smaller geographic footprint.

"It's not important to *just* have a handbook," says Wood. "It's important to have one that's really tailored to your business."

FAIRNESS FACTOR

Fairness is about having practical, easy-to-understand policies tailored to company operations, industry, and jurisdictional requirements.

Policies that are reasonable and easy to understand get followed. Employment experts skilled in surgically simplifying boilerplate language and customizing off-the-shelf employee handbooks can assist in making policies user-friendly.

But what's the point of following Policies if they're nonbinding guidance?

Interesting question. Focusing on the word *nonbinding* suggests an "anything goes" philosophy, inviting heavy reliance on management's positional power and equating it to unbridled authority. Yet the word *guidance* signifies direction and regulation, or a system of accountability, and a degree of consistency.

Indeed, Policies identify *what* employees are responsible for and *how* they are to be held responsible. They establish healthy boundaries to help manage employee expectations regarding conduct and processes. Their reasonableness, or health, is determined by how much they honor the covenants of good faith and fair dealing and Maslow's hierarchy of human motivational needs.

FAIRNESS FACTOR

Fairness is about having policies that establish healthy boundaries
to manage employee expectations and processes.

Although Policies play an important role in protecting employee engagement and satisfaction, they're only words. It's their implementation that governs the day-to-day employee experience and acts as the linchpin to employee engagement, satisfaction, and retention. Words are only as potent and effective as management's understanding of them and their steadfast ability to carry them out. Not surprisingly organizational dysfunction occurs when Policies are executed in a haphazard manner. The lack of commitment to consistently follow the rules allows the norms nobody wants to talk about to flourish and run rampant over healthy boundaries Policies seek to establish.

Commitment

Commitment to Policy compliance is what brings best business practices to life. After all, those procedures represent the methods that have been refined over time to create a proven glide path to more organizational success.

Unfortunately, the plain meaning and effectiveness of the simplest most beautifully crafted language can be neutralized by how they are interpreted and the behaviors they inspire. The former Soviet Union, for example, had word for word a more liberal Constitution than the United States. In practice, the narrow reading of those Soviet rights was repressive, and their citizens were left with less freedom than their American counterparts.

The ethics policy of Enron Corporation, the energy, commodities, and services company, is another example. It was heralded as a model for industry in its time. Enron's scandalous fall in 2001 due to shady accounting practices belied the policy's words. No executive would openly endorse flouting the law, yet some unwittingly sent that message through their actions, condoning a corporate culture of noncompliance that ultimately drove the company into bankruptcy, taking its Big Five accounting firm, Arthur Andersen, with it.

Both examples illustrate how organizational integrity gets subverted when leaders allow employees to ignore the letter and spirit of their governance documents.

FAIRNESS FACTOR

Fairness is about living up to the letter and spirit of
the organization's governance documents.

In my experience employees rarely plan to deliberately violate Policies. Instead, the Policies get ignored because employees don't know what's in them, don't understand them, or don't know how to apply them. Training and coaching can address those issues. They can generate more awareness, transparency, and understanding that makes the fairness of good faith and fair dealing come alive, and higher employee engagement, satisfaction, and retention attainable.

"Do the best you can until you know better.
Then when you know better, do better."
~MAYA ANGELOU

Knowledge management helps employees learn how to do better. It's a terrific way to stabilize the structural safety net and ensure fair and consistent policy implementation. It's particularly valuable for employees who are at a crossroads of transitioning from a contributor role to a management position. A Conference Board study found only 19% of middle managers received training in leadership and management, even though those jobs operate on the front lines of rank-and-file employee engagement. That unutilized 81% learning gap represents a substantial opportunity cost many organizations are failing to leverage.

------(**FAIRNESS FACTOR**)------

Fairness is about providing managers with the knowledge,
training, and coaching they need to support and
encourage greater employee engagement.

Knowledge management is how organizations make information available and develop employees. That's why it's not enough to simply hand a new hire an employee manual during their orientation or promote someone into a management position and expect seamless outcomes. Policy compliance is much easier when employees at all levels know why policies are in place and how to use them. Training and coaching help improve the judgment and confidence needed to do it consistently and fairly. They assist in sidestepping inconsistent Policy applications and disabling the norms nobody wants to talk about.

Knowledge Management and the Norms Nobody Wants to Talk About

When managers are unsure of how to handle a situation, they often avoid it until it escalates into a problem that's too big to hide. Now it's a crisis. The inability, or unwillingness, to provide constructive positive or negative feedback is a prime example. When left unchecked it gives free rein to two norms that nobody wants to talk about: a lack of recognition when they fail to acknowledge a job well done and poor conflict management when they sugarcoat or avert their eyes from subpar performance.

Fear leads many managers to avoid conflict, especially when conducting employee performance reviews. It's easier to tell someone their work meets expectations and *hope* they improve than providing concrete feedback about exactly what needs to change. Policies address that problem with a process for transforming hope into action. They provide procedures for documenting subpar performance and giving employees a chance to do better. Almost every handbook includes progressive disciplinary policies according to employment lawyer Mimi Soule. But not everyone knows how to use them properly.

The multistep process typically starts with a verbal warning; progresses through a written warning, written performance improvement plan, and employee suspension if things still don't improve; and ultimately ends in separation. If there's no clear understanding of *what* these warnings look like, *when* these warning should be issued, and especially *how* they should be documented, the organization can find itself in a hot mess.

Proper documentation demonstrates fairness in following Policies and gives people reasonable opportunities to improve their performance. Granted, there may be circumstances, including but not limited to fraud, theft, and serious safety violations that merit immediate dismissal. And while management certainly has the right to end an at-will employment relationship for any reason or no reason, such action is not necessarily free of legal liability exposure. It might still open the door to claims of illegal bias, retaliation, or wrongful termination if not handled properly. In extreme cases it could even create personal liability for individual managers. It all depends on the facts of a particular case. That's why accurately and objectively documenting employee performance is vitally important for all concerned.

FAIRNESS FACTOR

Fairness is about accurately documenting employee performance in valid and objective ways.

Now I need to be a lawyer, too? Seriously?

No. Not a lawyer. No bar exam is required, only some select legal literacy to appreciate how the company's Policies have been developed to comply with the law and are there for your protection. "Basic education and coaching on at least a few key procedures are what you want in place," according to Soule, particularly, "policies that are imperative to growing your business." These are namely hiring, onboarding, performance documentation, and offboarding to avoid legal claims.

Managers need to know how to transform Policies into action to empower more employee engagement, satisfaction, and retention. When paired with communication skills training to help managers handle difficult conversations, Policies become a vehicle for more collaboration and better teamwork. The ability to connect and interact with greater awareness of how our behavior affects employees can improve our approachability, help us to unlearn stereotypes and reduce our biases, and make us more cognizant of how we manage workloads—the other three norms nobody likes to talk about. Merely learning about Policies' existence does nothing more than allow them to collect dust on a shelf, a hard drive, or in the cloud; and turns compliance into another word for wishful thinking.

FAIRNESS FACTOR

Fairness is about cultivating the know-how needed to transform policies into action that empowers more employee engagement, satisfaction, and retention.

Policy Changes and Employee Buy-in

Sometimes management needs to change course. New policies need to be adopted, and old ones updated. Is education the answer to getting employee buy-in, too?

Yes, education in the form of smart messaging. Take, for example, the case of the new hotline policy.

When management announced the implementation of an anonymous employee hotline to report regulatory noncompliance at a manufacturing plant, the union employees called for a walkout.

Wow, that seems harsh. Why did they do that?

The workers labeled the hotline the "snitch line." They weren't convinced it was solely aimed at identifying and fixing regulatory noncompliance. They were suspicious of management's real intent and thought the compliance angle was fake. Not wanting to be part of a blame game that could lead to retaliation, the hotline got trashed. It was exactly the opposite policy outcome management wanted or needed.

A better communication strategy aimed at explaining why the hotline was being proposed, how regulatory noncompliance was hurting the business, how customers were leery of committing to large orders out of fear continued noncompliance would cause regulators to shut down the plant, which would in turn disrupt product delivery and upend supply chains, could have allayed employee fears. It would have clarified why the policy was being proposed *now* and why it was in everyone's interest to make the program a success. Educating employees in this way would have addressed their misconceptions and facilitated buy-in by aligning everyone's interests: compliance keeps the plant open, keeps workers employed, and keeps customers happy.

Soliciting Employee Feedback

A better communications plan that included tapping into existing company social networks to solicit employee feedback could have alerted management to how the union and the plant employees might react would have helped, too. These folks may not have positional power, but they're influencers because they're trusted, respected, and confided in by their peers. Since people support what they help create, listening to such feedback can improve employee buy-in. This gives them a voice and bolsters that important sense of belonging we explored earlier in our journey of seeking fairness at work that's essential to demonstrating good faith and fair dealing.

FAIRNESS FACTOR

Fairness is about giving employees a voice in new policy processes to facilitate buy-in and compliance.

So, is that all we need to improve employee engagement? Good policies supported by knowledge management and better messaging that includes employee feedback to get buy-in?

Not quite. The right set of Policies establishes the ground rules for protecting employee engagement, while educating and connecting with employees to obtain buy-in strengthens their commitment to follow them. Nonetheless, it's the organization's incentive structure that lights the fuse to ignite compliant behaviors or condones burning it down.

Incentive Structure

What gets rewarded gets done, and that means incentive structures promote action. Better employee engagement, satisfaction, and retention starts by looking at how the organization incentivizes behaviors that demonstrate good faith and fair dealing and asking whether what's being directly or indirectly remunerated supports the norms nobody wants to talk about. If it does, the organization is destabilizing its structural safety net by undermining the legitimacy of its governance documents.

────────── **FAIRNESS FACTOR** ──────────

Fairness is about creating incentives
that reward good faith and fair dealing.

Messaging plays a vital role in what employees hear and are incentivized to do. The most frequent and loudest calls to action are what get prioritized. If productivity, innovation, collaboration and all the other benefits of high employee engagement are truly important, how often is that message sent and the means of achieving it communicated to employees? How loud are those messages compared to the focus on business metrics solely tied to the bottom line? And how ironic is it that more employee engagement, the ticket to more productivity and a healthier bottom line, is relegated to being a distant understudy instead of having the starring role in the bottom-line show?

These questions require a humble look at the organization's reward system to determine whether what gets measured and rewarded represents a fully loaded cost that includes the impact of the counterproductive norms which hinder productivity. Those are the holes in the structural safety net that keep the organization from achieving its full cultural potential and that need mending if it wants to achieve greater employee engagement, retention and satisfaction.

Fairness is about being honest regarding the incentive structures
that keep the organization from achieving its full potential.

	Self-Awareness	Relationships	Accountability	Cultural Safety Net	Structural Safety Net
Unapproachability					
Unavailability Ignoring/Shunning Lack of Empathy	How We Present Ourselves	Curiosity Listening Growth Mindset	Deal Tending	Hiring Process On-Boarding Development	Governance Documents Commitment Incentives
Lack of Recognition					
Wage Theft Timely Compensation Subjective Rewards Credit Stealing No Feedback	How We're Perceived	Respect Gratitude Compassion	Deal Tending	Hiring Process On-Boarding Development	Governance Documents Commitment Incentives
Bias					
Microaggressions Bullying Discrimination Harassment	Our Internal Values and Beliefs	Attention Respect Self-Regulation Compassion	Deal Tending Deal Mending	Hiring Process On-Boarding Development	Governance Documents Commitment Incentives
Poor Conflict Management					
Volatility Conflict Avoidance Gaslighting Retaliation	How We Present Ourselves	Attention Respect Self-Regulation Compassion	Deal Mending	Hiring Process On-Boarding Development	Governance Documents Commitment Incentives
Poor Workload Management					
Unclear Communications Micromanaging Unrealistic Goals Lack of Support	How We're Perceived	Curiosity Listen Growth Mindset Attention Respect	Deal Making Deal Tending	Hiring Process On-Boarding Development	Governance Documents Commitment Incentives

Figure 8.4 How the Structural Safety Net Can Address the Norms Nobody Wants to Talk About

As illustrated in Figure 8.4, the structural safety net is last piece of the
5-part strategy that cracks the new code to more employee engagement,
satisfaction, and retention. Mending the structural safety net with
governance documents that include practical Policies, knowledge
management to empower more commitment to carrying them out, plus
an incentive structure designed to encourage compliance is another
way to tackle the norms nobody wants to talk about that squeeze the life
out of collaboration and innovation.

Little things can mean a lot when it comes to demonstrating good faith and fair dealing and building stronger workplace relationships. There is no one-size-fits-all solution. Employee-employer relationships are nuanced. Each component of the 5-part strategy, and indeed each fairness factor, can take on greater or lesser significance depending on the current state of a particular organization's culture. They are being offered as a way to reframe the age-old challenge of how to motivate and inspire employees that's being complicated by the evolving War for Talent.

To recap the fairness factors the structural safety net offers to influence perceptions of good faith and fair dealing, here's what they can teach us about improving employee engagement, retention, and satisfaction:

- ✓ Fairness is about consistent application of the organization's governance documents.

- ✓ Fairness is about policies being aligned with the organization's vision and mission statements.

- ✓ Fairness is about making sure all employees understand the organization's rules.

- ✓ Fairness is about making updated employee handbooks easily accessible to consistently communicate the organization's vision, mission, and key policies, programs, and procedures.

- ✓ Fairness is about adopting reasonable policies to create a system for the smooth functioning of the organization that demonstrates good faith and fair dealing.

✓ Fairness is about having policies and procedures that protect the physical and psychological safety of employees.

✓ Fairness is about having practical, easy-to-understand policies tailored to company operations, industry, and jurisdictional requirements.

✓ Fairness is about having policies that establish healthy boundaries to manage employee expectations and processes.

✓ Fairness is about living up to the letter and spirit of the organization's governance documents.

✓ Fairness is about providing managers with the knowledge, training, and coaching they need to support and encourage greater employee engagement.

✓ Fairness is about accurately documenting employee performance in valid and objective ways.

✓ Fairness is about cultivating the know-how needed to transform policies into action that empowers more employee engagement, satisfaction, and retention.

✓ Fairness is about giving employees a voice in new policy processes to facilitate buy-in and compliance.

✓ Fairness is about creating incentives that reward good faith and fair dealing.

✓ Fairness is about being honest regarding the incentive structures that keep the organization from achieving its full potential.

✓ Fairness is about taking action to remedy the norms nobody wants to talk about.

Someone who shared my frustration at a past job once asked, "How do you explain what's wrong with this place to someone on the outside?" I shrugged my shoulders. The injustices were continuous, some subtle and some not so subtle. Watching the chaos and being subject to it was the proverbial Death by a Thousand Cuts. Organizational cultures like this happen when (1) those in authority turn a blind eye to the norms nobody wants to talk about, (2) employees raising concerns experience retaliation, and (3) workers are intimidated into obeying and conforming. It's a radioactive fear-based culture and a doom loop for employee engagement, satisfaction, and retention.

The unfairness and fear that permeates such organizations is akin to the "invisible gorilla." A famous 1990s experiment of the same name involve three people wearing white tee shirts and three wearing black ones passing a basketball between themselves. Volunteers are asked to silently count the number of passes between players in white. But part way through the action someone in a gorilla suit slowly walks across the court, beats their chest, and exits the room. Afterwards, when asked about the gorilla, half the volunteers didn't see it. They were too busy following the basketball, counting passes, and being focused on counting accurately. Their selective attention made the gorilla invisible.

A similar phenomenon happens in businesses. When management's attention is consumed by numbers and managing up the chain of command, or for business owners managing customers, clients, or patients, they literally don't "see" the norms nobody wants to talk about or how they affect their staff. However, the powerful gorilla hiding in plain view is definitely visible to employees. They feel it's hot breath and crushing weight every day. It detracts from their job satisfaction. Low employee engagement and retention follows. Such employee reactions are a *reasonable response* to the monkey business. They're not independent of it.

Fairness Is a Management and Leadership Imperative

Fairness is what drives cooperation and productivity. That's why cracking the new code of greater employee engagement, retention, and satisfaction starts with recognizing the crucial role leadership's self-awareness and empathy plays in establishing fairness at work.

Humans are social beings. There is an implied social contract in *all* of our relationships that require good faith and fair dealing. Family. Friends. Colleagues. Acquaintances. Workplace relationships are no exception.

We expect people to be honest and to reasonably protect our physical and psychological safety. When they don't, our trust is damaged, and we're less inclined to cooperate. We keep our distance. Being paid wages does not create an exemption. It merely stretches our patience with the financial need. It compels us to obey and conform.

We also expect people to engage in fair dealing and not unreasonably interfere or hamper our ability to contribute and belong. When they do, it disrupts our ability to connect with others. We become estranged and less willing to invest extra effort in those relationships.

Hope for the Future

The need for fairness is simply an immutable part of human nature. Recognizing that fact, exercising more self-awareness of the employee experience, and demonstrating empathy are ways leaders can successfully manage employee expectations and perceptions of fairness.

As described in the preceding chapters, there are five pathways to empowering and enabling an environment that allows employees to do their best work: trust building, relationship chemistry, genuine accountability, the cultural safety net, and the structural safety net.

What these five routes have in common is an unwavering focus on the covenants of good faith and fair dealing in the implied social contract.

Strategy for Seeking Fairness at Work

Little things can and do mean a lot. That's why I've identified over 100 Fairness Factors for readers to consider. It's a guide to small changes that can have a positive effect. Identifying which one, or which combination, will yield the biggest improvement for a specific organization requires a candid look at an individual organization's existing culture.

> *"Big doors swing on little hinges."*
> W. CLEMENT STONE

As a practical matter, fairness is ultimately a test of leadership character. It takes honesty to acknowledge the norms nobody wants to talk about, humility to admit they're problematic, courage to craft meaningful solutions, and persistence to reliably implement them in a way that puts the best interests of the entire organization first.

While such discipline may ruffle certain privileged feathers, organizations that are serious about wanting to be competitive and attract the best talent can't afford the costs associated with disengaged employees or unwanted workforce turnover.

They not only can do better. They must do better to thrive in today's economy.

Reexamining the exercise of power in organizations and tackling the invisible gorilla offers a path forward. Fairness is not about losing control and giving everybody what they want. The covenants of good faith and fair dealing at the heart of fairness focus on protecting *reasonable* human needs of honesty, safety, esteem, and belonging. They respect our *shared* humanity. And doing that requires taking both sides of the implied employee-employer social contract into account.

Fairness at work is the *real* driving force behind the financial bottom line. Infusing more fairness into the workplace is therefore a leadership superpower and a journey *Seeking Fairness at Work* has demystified by bringing to light the employee perspective and translating the abstract concept of fairness into practical, morally sound principles, identifiable standards, and proven action steps.

POSTSCRIPT

Interested in more?

VISIT Seeking FairnessAtWork.com

DOWNLOAD *Elevating Leadership Through Fairness:*
26 No Nonsense Tips to Boost Employee Engagement –
a free bonus chapter available at
SeekingFairnessAtWork.com/bonus-chapter

ALSO, if you enjoyed this book, I'd be honored if you'd post a great review on Amazon or Goodreads. Mention something that you really liked about the book and why.
The most impactful reviews are short and succinct.

ENDNOTES

Introduction

Aten, Jamie; Our Psychology, Not Pay is Driving the Great Resignation; Oct. 8, 2021; https://www.smerconish.com/exclusive-content/our-psychology-not-pay-is-driving-the-great-resignation.

Bryner, Jeanna; Abused Workers Fight Back by Slacking Off; Live Science, October 8, 2007.

Clifton, Jim, and Jim Harter, *It's the Manager*, Gallup Press (2019).

Decision-wise, The ROI of Employee Engagement: Show Me the Money!; 2021; https://decision-wise.com/show-me-the-money-the-roi-of-employee-engagement/.

Ellis, Lindsay and Ray A. Smith; "Your Coworkers Are Less Ambitious; Bosses Adjust to the New Order," *The Wall Street Journal*, December 31, 2022; https://www.wsj.com/articles/your-coworkers-are-less-ambitious-bosses-adjust-to-the-new-order-11672441067?st=pmkf1rr58 7ggki8&reflink=desktopwebshare_permalink.

Evanish, Jason; Why People Leave Managers, Not Companies (and what to do about it), Get Lighthouse Blog, https://getlighthouse.com/blog/people-leave-managers-not-companies/.

Fuller, J., & Kerr, W. The great resignation didn't start with the pandemic. Harvard Business Review, March 23, 2022; https://hbr.org/2022/03/the-great-resignation-didnt-start-with-the-pandemic.

Gallup, *State of the Global Workplace Report: 2022 Report*, Gallup Press (2022).

Gallup, *State of the Global Workplace Report: 2023 Report*, Gallup Press (2023).

Johnson, Akilah and Charlotte Gomez, Stress is Weathering Our Bodies From the Inside Out, *Washington Post*, Dec. 6, 2023, https://www.washingtonpost.com/health/interactive/2023/stress-chronic-illness-aging/?itid=sr_1.

Morrison, E.W., Employee Voice and Silence, Annual Review of Organizational Psychology and Organizational Behavior, Volume 1, 2014, pp.173-197.

Moyer, Melinda Wenner, Your Body Knows You're Burned Out, *The New York Times,* June 22, 2023; https://www.nytimes.com/2022/02/15/well/live/burnout-work-stress.html.

Pinsker, Joe; Why People Get the "Sunday Scaries," *The Atlantic*, February 9, 2020, https://www.theatlantic.com/family/archive/2020/02/sunday-scaries-anxiety-workweek/606289/.

Saleem, Z., Shenbei, Z., & Hanif, A. M. (2020). Workplace Violence and Employee Engagement: The Mediating Role of Work Environment and Organizational Culture. SAGE Open, 10(2). https://doi.org/10.1177/2158244020935885.

Tong, Goh Chiew; "1 in 5 employees are 'loud quitting.' Here's why it's worse than 'quiet quitting;" June 27, 2023, https://www.cnbc.com/2023/06/28/employees-are-now-loud-quitting-heres-why-its-worse-than-quiet-quitting.html.

Torres, Monica; This is What Happens to Your Body When You hate Your Job, Huffington Post, January 21, 2019.

Wong, Kellie; Understanding the Power Behind Employee Happiness; Last updated January 21, 2020; https://www.achievers.com/blog/why-you-cant-afford-disengaged-employees/.

Chapter 1

Allen, Dr. Kelly-Ann and Associate Professor Peggy Kern, The Importance of Belonging Across Life, *Psychology Today*, June 20, 2019; https://www.psychologytoday.com/us/blog/sense-belonging/201906/the-importance-belonging-across-life.

Angell, Melissa, The Real Reasons Workers Are Leaving in Droves? (Burnout Is on the List, but Not at the Top), *Inc.com*, January 25, 2022, https://www.inc.com/melissa-angell/great-resignation-burnout-workers-upskilling-career-development.html#:~:text=91%20percent%3A%20I%20wanted%20to,was%20growing%20in%20my%20position

Ballou, Nichole Simone, "The Effects of Psychological Contract Breach on Job Outcomes" (2013). Master's Theses. 4327. DOI: https://doi.org/10.31979/etd.sqy9-u9df https://scholarworks.sjsu.edu/etd_theses/4327.

BetterUp, The Connection Crisis: Why Community Matters in the New World of Work, 2022; https://grow.betterup.com/resources/build-a-culture-of-connection-report.

Bryner, Jeanna; Abused Workers Fight Back by Slacking Off; *LiveScience*, October 8, 2007; https://www.livescience.com/1929-abused-workers-fight-slacking.html.

Carr, Evan W., Andrew Reece, Gabriella Rosen Kellerman, and Alexi Robichaux, The Value of Belonging at Work, *Harvard Business Review*, December 16, 2019; https://hbr.org/2019/12/the-value-of-belonging-at-work.

Clifton, Jim, and Jim Harter, *It's the Manager*, Gallup Press (2019).

Cook, Gareth, Why We Are Wired to Connect, *Scientific American*, October 22, 2013; https://www.scientificamerican.com/article/why-we-are-wired-to-connect/.

Gale, Sarah Fister, The New Employer-Employee Social Contract, *Chief Learning Officer*, May 8, 2017; https://www.chieflearningofficer.com/2017/05/08/employer-employee-social-contract-2/.

Kelly, Catherine Pastrikos, What You Should Know about the Implied Duty of Good Faith and Fair Dealing, American Bar Association Practice Points, July 26, 2016, https://www.americanbar.org/groups/litigation/committees/business-torts-unfair-competition/practice/2016/duty-of-good-faith-fair-dealing/.

Lubin Austermuehle, Difference Between Implied Covenant of Good Faith and Fair Dealing and the Fiduciary Duty of Good Faith, https://www.thebusinesslitigators.com/difference-between-implied-covenant-of-good-faith-and-fair-deali.html#:~:text=Notably%2C%20the%20implied%20covenant%20of,subject%20to%20the%20implied%20covenant.

Maslow, Abraham, A Theory of Human Motivation, *Psychological Review*, 50, 370-396 (1943).

McCarthy, Jeremy, The Social Contract at Work, *Psychology of Wellbeing*, October 18, 2011,

Reece, Andrew, David Yaden, Gabriella Kellerman, Alexi Robichaux, Rebecca Goldstein, Barry Schwartz, Martin Seligman & Roy Baumeister (2021) Mattering is an Indicator of Organizational Health and Employee Success, *The Journal of Positive Psychology*, 16:2, 228-248, DOI: 10.1080/17439760.2019.1689416

Riordan, Christine M. and Kevin O'Brien, For Great Teamwork, Start with a Social Contract, *Harvard Business Review*, April 17, 2012, https://hbr.org/2012/04/to-ensure-great-teamwork-start.

Rousseau, Denise M., Psychological and Implied Contracts in Organizations, *Employee Responsibilities and Rights Journal*, June 1, 1989; https://doi.org/10.1007/BF01384942.

Schiller, Ben, We Need a new Social Contract Between Workers, Companies, and Society: Here Are Some Ideas, *Fast Company*, July 18, 2016; https://www.fastcompany.com/3061047/we-need-a-new-social-contract-between-workers-companies-and-society-here-are-some-ideas.

Werby, Olga, Health, Human Rights, and Maslow's Hierarchy of Needs, Interfaces Blog, September 15, 2013; https://interfaces.com/blog/2013/09/health-human-rights-and-maslows-hierarchy-of-needs/.

Chapter 2

Aasland, Merethe Schanke, and Anders Skogstad, Guy Notelaers, Morten Birkeland Nielsen, Ståle Einarsen; The Prevalence of Destructive Leadership Behavior, *British Journal of Management*, May 25, 2010; https://onlinelibrary.wiley.com/doi/abs/10.1111/j.1467-8551.2009.00672.x

Asch, Solomon E.; Opinions and Social Pressure, *Scientific American*, November 1955.

Berlin, Gretchen; Meredith Lapointe, and Mhoire Murphy, *Increased workforce turnover and pressures straining provider operations*, August 19, 2021; https://www.mckinsey.com/industries/healthcare-systems-and-services/our-insights/increased-workforce-turnover-and-pressures-straining-provider-operations.

Brock Bastian & Nick Haslam (2011): Experiencing Dehumanization: Cognitive and Emotional Effects of Everyday Dehumanization, Basic and Applied Social Psychology, 33:4, 295-303; https://www2.psy.uq.edu.au/~uqbbast1/Bastian%20&%20Haslam%20BASP%202011.pdf.

Carr, Evan W. Andrew Reece, Gabriella Rosen Kellerman and Alexi Robichaux; The Value of Belonging at Work, *Harvard Business Review*, December 16, 2019.

Domonoske, Camila, 'Disgruntled Employee' At Orlando Business Kills 5 People, Authorities Say, NPR, June 5, 2017; https://www.npr.org/sections/thetwo-way/2017/06/05/531578459/disgruntled-employee-at-orlando-business-kills-5-people-police-say.

Fiske, S. T. (2001). Effects of power on bias: Power explains and maintains individual, group, and societal disparities. In A. Y. Lee-Chai & J. A. Bargh (Eds.), *The use and abuse of power: Multiple perspectives on the causes of corruption* (pp. 181–193). Psychology Press.

Gregory, Scott, The Most Common Type of Incompetent Leader, *Harvard Business Review*, March 30, 2018; https://hbr.org/2018/03/the-most-common-type-of-incompetent-leader.

Groysberg, Boris and Jeremiah Lee, Jesse Price, and J. Yo-Jud Cheng; The Culture Factor, *Harvard Business Review*, January – February 2018; https://hbr.org/2018/01/the-culture-factor.

Hasl-Kelchner, Hanna. "Are You Accidentally Self-Sabotaging Your Business or Career Success?" *Business Confidential Now with Hanna Hasl-Kelchner.* Podcast audio. March 31, 2022. https://businessconfidentialradio.com/Are-you-accidentally-self-sabotaging-business-or-career-success.

Henrich, J. and F. Gil-White; The evolution of prestige. *Evolution and Human Behavior,* 22, 165–196. (2001).

King's College of London, History of Moral Injury, YouTube video, 2021; https://youtu.be/QX8_QkNUoy8?si=EtYQRYqZUlE7tzjw.

Kirsch, Nancy, It's Not Burnout! It is Moral Injury: Why Should Regulators be Concerned?; The Federation of State Boards of Physical Therapy, 2020; https://www.fsbpt.org/Free-Resources/FSBPT-Forum/Forum-2021/Its-Not-Burnout-It-is-Moral-Injury-Why-Should-Regulators-be-Concerned#:~:text=Those%20factors%20result%20in%20moral,care%20and%20protect%20the%20public.

Last Week Tonight with John Oliver. 2022. Year. Season #9, Episode #6, "Trucks." Directed by Paul Pennolino. April 3, 2022, on HBO.

Meyersohn, Nathaniel, Workers Don't Know Their Schedules Until the Last Minute. Big Problem, CNN Business, Updated January 30, 2022, https://www.cnn.com/2022/01/28/economy/retail-fast-food-workers-jobs-schedules/index.html

Milgram, Stanley; Obedience to Authority, Harper Perennial Modern Classics; Reissue edition (August 6, 2019).

Namie, Gary and Ruth, 2021 WBI U.S. Workplace Bullying Survey, Workplace Bullying Institute, June 2023; https://workplacebullying.org/wp-content/uploads/2023/06/2021-Full-Report.pdf.

Newman, Andy and Ray Rivera, Fed-Up Flight Attendant Makes Sliding Exit, The New York Times, August 9, 2010; https://www.nytimes.com/2010/08/10/nyregion/10attendant.html.

Pfeffer, Jeffrey; *Dying for a Paycheck*, Harper Business (2018).

Praslova, Ludila and Ron Carucci, Caroline Stokes, How Bullying Manifests at Work – and How to Stop It, *Harvard Business Review*, November 4, 2022; https://hbr.org/2022/11/how-bullying-manifests-at-work-and-how-to-stop-it.

Shaw, Alex, Vivian Li, and Kristina Olson; Children Apply Principles of Physical Ownership to Ownership of Ideas, *Cognitive Science* (2012).

Williamson, Victoria; Dominic Murphy, *Moral injury: the effect on mental health and implications for treatment*; June 1, 2021; https://kclpure.kcl.ac.uk/portal/en/publications/moral-injury(030995cb-c84a-48a5-bb17-a6cfa30a6a2b).html.

Chapter 3

Alda, Alan, *If I Understood You, Would I Have This Look on My Face?*, Random House (2018).

Baer, Drake, "Powerful People Think Differently About Their Thoughts," *The Cut*, October 27, 2016. https://www.thecut.com/2016/10/how-powerful-people-think-differently.html

Battilana, Julie and Tiziana Casciaro; *Power, for All;* Simon & Schuster (2021).

Botwin, Andy; Power vs Influence: How Can it Make or Break Your Organization, Strategy People Culture Blog, October 3, 2022, https://www.strategypeopleculture.com/blog/power-vs-influence/.

Briñol, P., Petty, R. E., Valle, C., Rucker, D. D., & Becerra, A. (2007). The effects of message recipients' power before and after persuasion: A self-validation analysis. Journal of Personality and Social Psychology, 93(6), 1040–1053. https://doi.org/10.1037/0022-3514.93.6.1040

Covey, Stephen M.R.; *The Speed of Trust*, Free Press, 2018.

Goleman, Daniel, *Emotional Intelligence: Why It Can Matter More than IQ*, Bantam; Revised edition 2006.

Goleman, Daniel, "Rich People Just Care Less," *New York Times*, October 5, 2013, https://archive.nytimes.com/opinionator.blogs. nytimes.com/2013/10/05/rich-people-just-care-less/

Harter, Jim, "U.S. Employee Engagement Needs a Rebound in 2023," January 25, 2023, Gallup.com, https://www.gallup.com/ workplace/468233/employee-engagement-needs-rebound-2023. aspx#:~:text=The%20good%20news%20is%20this,even%20 during%20highly%20disruptive%20times.

Hasl-Kelchner, Hanna, *The Business Guide to Legal Literacy*, Jossey-Bass 2006.

Hasl-Kelchner, Hanna. "Keys to Unlock Employee Loyalty." *Business Confidential Now with Hanna Hasl-Kelchner*. Podcast audio. March 16, 2017. https://businessconfidentialradio.com/keys-to-unlock-employee-loyalty/.

Hasl-Kelchner, Hanna. "Managing the Millennial Mid-Career Culture Clash With Kelly Waffle." *Business Confidential Now with Hanna Hasl-Kelchner*. Podcast audio. January 12, 2023. https:// businessconfidentialradio.com/millennial-mid-career-culture-clash-with-kelly-waffle/.

Herring, Claire, Three Reasons Leaders Are not more Inclusive and How to Help, Association for Talent Development Blog, March 19, 2021; https://www.td.org/atd-blog/three-reasons-leaders-are-not-more-inclusive-and-how-to-help.

Hinge Research Institute, Culture Clash: The Employee Experience Problem and How to Fix it, 2022; https://hingemarketing.com/library/ article/culture-clash-the-employee-experience-problem-and-how-to-fix-it.

Hinge Research Institute, Navigating the Mid-Career Talent Crisis: A Report for the Professional Services, 2022; https://hingemarketing. com/library/article/navigating-the-mid-career-talent-crisis-a-report-for-the-professional-services

Hogeveen, Jeremy, Michael Inzlicht, and Sukhvinder Obhi. "Power changes how the brain responds to others." *Journal of Experimental Psychology:* General 143, no. 2 (April 2014): 755-62. doi.org/10.1037/a0033477.

Ibarra, Herminia, The Authenticity Paradox, *Harvard Business Review,* January-February 2015, https://hbr.org/2015/01/the-authenticity-paradox.

Kanter, Rosabeth Moss, Power Failure in Management Circuits, *Harvard Business Review,* July 1979.

Keltner, Dacher, Don't Let Power Corrupt You, *Harvard Business Review*, October 2016, https://hbr.org/2016/10/dont-let-power-corrupt-you.

Keltner, Dacher, *The Power Paradox: How We Gain and Lose Influence,* Penguin Books 2018.

Keltner D, Gruenfeld DH, Anderson C. Power, approach, and inhibition. *Psychol Rev.* 2003 Apr;110(2):265-84. doi: 10.1037/0033-295x.110.2.265. PMID: 12747524.

Koval, P., Laham, S. M., Haslam, N., Bastian, B., & Whelan, J. A. (2012). Our Flaws Are More Human Than Yours: Ingroup Bias in Humanizing Negative Characteristics. Personality and Social Psychology Bulletin, 38(3), 283–295. https://doi.org/10.1177/0146167211423777.

Kraus, Michael, Psychology Suggests that Power Doesn't Make People Bad – It Just Reveals Their True Natures, Quartz, October 14, 2016; https://qz.com/809580/psychology-shows-that-the-more-power-we-give-to-people-like-donald-trump-the-worse-they-get.

Kraus, Michael W., Serena Chen, Dacher Keltner; The power to be me: Power elevates self-concept consistency and authenticity, *Journal of Experimental Social Psychology,* Vol 47, Issue 5, 2011, Pages 974-980, https://doi.org/10.1016/j.jesp.2011.03.017

Love, Scott, *Why They Follow: How to Lead with Positive Influence,* CreateSpace Independent Publishing Platform (2015).

Ratliff, Jill, *Leadership Through Trust and Collaboration,* Morgan James Publishing (2020).

Stillman, Jessica, Science: Powerful People Really Do Think Differently From the Rest of Us, Inc Magazine, November 3, 2016, https://www.inc.com/jessica-stillman/science-powerful-people-really-do-think-differently-than-the-rest-of-us.html.

Vredenburgh, Donald, and Yael Brender. "The Hierarchical Abuse of Power in Work Organizations." *Journal of Business Ethics* 17, no. 12 (1998): 1337–47. http://www.jstor.org/stable/25073966.

Zak, Jaul, The Neuroscience of Trust, Harvard Business Review, January – February 2017, https://hbr.org/2017/01/the-neuroscience-of-trust.

Chapter 4

ADP Research Institute, Employee Satisfaction vs. Employee Engagement: Are They the Same Thing?, 2012; https://www.adp.com/~/media/ri/whitepapers/employee%20engagement%20vs%20employee%20satisfaction%20white%20paper.ashx#:~:text=The%20answer%20is%20no.,actionable%20insights%20into%20the%20workforce.

Argandona, A. (2015). Humility in management. *Journal of Business Ethics*, 132(1), 63–71. https://doi.org/10.1007/s10551-014-2311-8.

Barsade, Sigal G., Constantinos G.V. Coutifaris, and Julianna Pillemer; Emotional Contagion in Organizational Life, *Research in Organizational Behavior,* Vol. 38, 2018, Pages 137-151; https://www.sciencedirect.com/science/article/abs/pii/S0191308518300108.

Bernstein, Jeffrey and Susan Magee, *Why Can't You Read My Mind?* Da Capo Press 2004.

Catalano, Rob, Is Your Employee Survey Approach Stuck in 2019? Four Employee Listening Trends For 2022, *Forbes,* January 31, 2022; https://www.forbes.com/sites/forbeshumanresourcescouncil/2022/01/31/is-your-employee-survey-approach-stuck-in-2019-four-employee-listening-trends-for-2022/?sh=432066d07a0f.

Carucci, Ron and Dorie Clark, 4 Surprising Ways of Earning – and Keeping – Others' Trust, *Fast Company,* February 23, 2022; https://www.fastcompany.com/90723426/4-surprising-ways-of-earning-and-keeping-others-trust.

Clifton, Jim, and Jim Harter, *It's the Manager,* Gallup Press (2019).

Deloitte, The Bias Barrier, 2019 State of Inclusion Survey, https://www2.deloitte.com/content/dam/Deloitte/us/Documents/about-deloitte/inclusion-survey-research-the-bias-barrier.pdf

Grant, Adam, The Fine Line Between Helpful and Harmful Authenticity, *New York Times*, April 10, 2020, https://www.nytimes.com/2020/04/10/smarter-living/the-fine-line-between-helpful-and-harmful-authenticity.html.

Hasl-Kelchner, Hanna. "How to Reliably Improve Workplace Trust and Collaboration with Jill Ratliff." *Business Confidential Now with Hanna Hasl-Kelchner.* Podcast audio. July 6, 2023. https://businessconfidentialradio.com/reliably-improve-workplace-trust-and-collaboration-with-Jill-Ratliff

Hasl-Kelchner, Hanna. "Why Humility is the Secret Weapon of Effective Leadership." *Business Confidential Now with Hanna Hasl-Kelchner.* Podcast audio. June 2, 2022. https://businessconfidentialradio.com/why-humility-secret-weapon-effective-leadership.

Hasl-Kelchner, Hanna. "Why Self-Awareness in Business Leadership is Critically Important." *Business Confidential Now with Hanna Hasl-Kelchner.* Podcast audio. May 5, 2022. https://businessconfidentialradio.com/why-self-awareness-in-business-leadership-is-critically-important/.

Heffernan, Margaret; *Willful Blindness: Why We Ignore the Obvious at Our Peril*, Walker & Company (2011).

Lencioni, Patrick; *The Five Dysfunctions of a Team*, Jossey-Bass (2002).

McGaugh, James L., Making lasting memories: Remembering the significant, *The Proceedings of the National Academy of Sciences,* Vol. 110 (supplement_2) 10402-10407, June 10, 2013, https://doi.org/10.1073/pnas.1301209110.

Nielsen, Rob, and Jennifer A. Marrone. "Humility: Our current understanding of the construct and its role in organizations." *International Journal of Management Reviews* 20, no. 4 (2018): 805-824.

Ratliff, Jill, *Leadership Through Trust and Collaboration,* Morgan James Publishing 2020.

Reece, Andrew and David Yaden, Gabriella Kellerman, Alexi Robichaux, Rebecca Goldstein, Barry Schwartz, Martin Seligman & Roy Baumeister (2021) Mattering is an indicator of organizational health and employee success, *The Journal of Positive Psychology*, 16:2, 228-248, DOI: 10.1080/17439760.2019.1689416

Taylor, Jill Bolte, *My Stroke of Insight*, Viking Adult 2007.

Weber, Chelsea, 8 Reasons Your Employee Engagement Survey Isn't Working, Gotham Culture Blog, March 30, 2017; https://gothamculture.com/2017/03/30/8-reasons-your-employee-engagement-survey-isnt-working/.

Wiles, Jackie, Is It Time to Throw Out Your Old Employee Engagement Survey?, Nov. 26, 2018, https://www.gartner.com/smarterwithgartner/is-it-time-to-toss-out-your-old-employee-engagement-survey.

Chapter 5

Barsade, Sigal G., Constantinos G.V. Coutifaris, and Julianna Pillemer; Emotional Contagion in Organizational Life, *Research in Organizational Behavior,* Vol. 38, 2018, Pages 137-151; https://www.sciencedirect.com/science/article/abs/pii/S0191308518300108.

Baum, Anne Corley, *Small Mistakes, Big Consequences: Develop Your Soft Skills to Help You Succeed*, Momosa Publishing, LLC 2019.

Berinato, Scott, Negative Feedback Rarely Leads to Improvement, *Harvard Business Review*, January–February 2018 Issue, https://hbr.org/2018/01/negative-feedback-rarely-leads-to-improvement.

Fuhrmans, Vanessa and Joseph Pisani, "A Rallying Cry or a Rant? 'Pity City' CEO Comments Show Perils of Video Meetings," The Wall Street Journal, April 21, 2023; https://www.wsj.com/articles/a-rallying-cry-or-a-rant-pity-city-ceo-comments-show-perils-of-video-meetings-2a95d0b1

Goleman, Daniel, *Emotional Intelligence: Why It Can Matter More than IQ*, Bantam; Revised edition 2006.

Hasl-Kelchner, Hanna. "Effective Listening – The Secret to Powerful Communications with Dr. Kittie Watson." *Business Confidential Now with Hanna Hasl-Kelchner*. Podcast audio. July 28, 2022. https://businessconfidentialradio.com/effective-listening-the-secret-to-powerful-communications-with-dr-kittie-watson/

Hasl-Kelchner, Hanna. "How to Constructively Confront Difficult Conversations in the Workplace." *Business Confidential Now with Hanna Hasl-Kelchner*. Podcast audio. December 10, 2020. https://businessconfidentialradio.com/constructively-confront-difficult-conversations-in-the-workplace/

Hasl-Kelchner, Hanna. "Improve Your Communications With These Powerful Media Interview Tips." *Business Confidential Now with Hanna Hasl-Kelchner*. Podcast audio. August 26, 2021. https://businessconfidentialradio.com/improve-your-communications-with-powerful-media-interview-tips/

Hasl-Kelchner, Hanna. "How Improvisation Skills Can Make You a Better Leaders." *Business Confidential Now with Hanna Hasl-Kelchner*. Podcast audio. May 20, 2021. https://businessconfidentialradio.com/improvisation-skills-make-better-leader/

Hasl-Kelchner, Hanna. "Improving Remote Business Communication By Bringing Back Humanity With Dr. Diane Lennard." *Business Confidential Now with Hanna Hasl-Kelchner.* Podcast audio. December 22, 2022. https://businessconfidentialradio.com/improving-remote-business-communication-by-bringing-back-humanity-with-dr-diane-lennard

Hasl-Kelchner, Hanna. "Soft Skill Secrets That Are Essential to Workplace Trust." *Business Confidential Now with Hanna Hasl-Kelchner.* Podcast audio. May 13, 2021. https://businessconfidentialradio.com/soft-skill-secrets-essential-workplace-trust/.

Hasl-Kelchner, Hanna. "Why Self-Awareness in Business Leadership is Critically Important." *Business Confidential Now with Hanna Hasl-Kelchner.* Podcast audio. May 5, 2022. https://businessconfidentialradio.com/why-self-awareness-in-business-leadership-is-critically-important/.

Howard, Steven, *Better Decisions, Better Thinking, Better Outcomes,* Caliente Press 2018.

Innolect – Employee Retention and Listening Architecture; October 4, 2022, https://www.youtube.com/watch?v=t793LHh_OR8

Isidore, Chris. "CEO questions whether parents who are primary caregivers are being 'fair' to employers and children," CNN, April 20, 2023. https://www.cnn.com/2023/04/20/business/ceo-questions-parenting-vs-work/index.html

Maybin, Sarita. *If You Can't Say Anything Nice, What Do You Say?: Practical Solutions For Working Together Better.* BookSurge, 2006.

Pentland, Alex "Sandy", The New Science of Building Great Teams, *Harvard Business Review,* April 2012, https://hbr.org/2012/04/the-new-science-of-building-great-teams.

Reiss, Helen, *The Empathy Effect,* Sounds True 2018.

Tannen, Deborah, *Talking From 9 to 5: How Women's and Men's Conversational Styles Affect Who Gets Heard, Who Gets Credit and What Gets Done at Work,* Morrow, 1994.

Tannen, Deborah, *That's Not What I Meant! How Conversational Style Makes or Breaks Relationships,* Harper 1986.

Watson, Kittie W. and Larry L. Barker, *Listen Up Second Edition,* Trafford, 2014.

Zaki, Jamil, *The War for Kindness: Building Empathy in a Fractured World,* Broadway Books 2020.

Chapter 6

Dattner, Ben, Most Work Conflicts Aren't Due to Personality, *Harvard Business Review,* May 20, 2014, https://hbr.org/2014/05/most-work-conflicts-arent-due-to-personality.

Eikenberg, Darcy, Why Your Senior-Level new Hire Isn't Working Out, Talent Management, https://www.talentmgt.com/articles/2023/09/11/why-your-senior-level-new-hire-isnt-working-out/?utm_medium=email&_hsmi=273832392&_hsenc=p2ANqtz-9DkCgT_Ddv5ei0u7VxfvMzkEUXDScXDzV77TfVQyPD1wuhDk Jv7pjj13T9TMJ4OH0DIcqiHN8PZEqNI6DkQdS-tyF6BQ&utm_content=273831654&utm_source=hs_email

Hasl-Kelchner, Hanna, *The Business Guide to Legal Literacy: What Every Manager Should Know About the Law,* Jossey-Bass (2006).

Hasl-Kelchner, Hanna. "How to Improve the Strategic Value of Workplace Violence Prevention with Felix Nater" *Business Confidential Now with Hanna Hasl-Kelchner.* Podcast audio. June 1, 2023. https://businessconfidentialradio.com/how-to-improve-strategic-value-workplace-violence-prevention-with-Felix-Nater

Hasl-Kelchner, Hanna. "How Smart Leaders Successfully Conquer Fear of Conflict at Work with Dr Debra Dupree" *Business Confidential Now with Hanna Hasl-Kelchner.* Podcast audio. April 20, 2023. https://businessconfidentialradio.com/how-smart-leaders-successfully-conquer-fear-of-conflict-at-work-with-dr-debra-dupree

Huffington, Ariana, Give Compassionate Feedback While Still Being Constructive, *New York Times*, February 26, 2020. https://www.nytimes.com/2020/02/24/smarter-living/how-to-give-helpful-feedback.html.

Kusy, Mitchell, *Why I Don't Work Here Anymore: A Leader's Guide to Offset the Financial and Emotional Costs of Toxic Employees*, CRC Press (2018).

Lind, E. A. (1997). Litigation and claiming in organizations: Antisocial behavior or quest for justice? In R. A. Giacalone & J. Greenberg (Eds.), Antisocial behavior in organizations (pp. 150–171). Sage Publications, Inc.

Lipman, Victor; 66% Of Employees Would Quit If They Feel Unappreciated, *Forbes*, April 15, 2017; https://www.forbes.com/sites/victorlipman/2017/04/15/66-of-employees-would-quit-if-they-feel-unappreciated/#35a049026897.

Paterson, Kerry, Joseph Grenny, Ron McMillan, Al Switzler, *Crucial Confrontations*, McGraw Hill (2005).

Porath, Christine L., Alexandra Gerbasi, Sebastian L Schorch, The Effects of Civility on Advice, Leadership, and Performance, *Journal of Applied Psychology*, September 2015.

Schaerer, Michael and Roderick Swaab, Are You Sugarcoating Your Feedback Without Realizing It? *Harvard Business Review*, October 08, 2019, https://hbr.org/2019/10/are-you-sugarcoating-your-feedback-without-realizing-it.

Schwarz, Roger, The "Sandwich Approach" Undermines Your Feedback, *Harvard Business Review*, April 19, 2013, https://hbr.org/2013/04/the-sandwich-approach-undermin.

Seifert, Matthias and Joel Brockner, Emily C. Bianchi, and Henry Moon, How Workplace Fairness Affects Employee Commitment, *MIT Sloan Management Review*, November 5, 2015, https://sloanreview.mit.edu/article/how-workplace-fairness-affects-employee-commitment/.

Voss, Chris, *Never Split the Difference: Negotiating As If Your Life Depended on It*, VOSS/RAZ (2017).

Wiest, Brianna; 64% Of New Hires Will Leave Their Jobs Because Of This Experience, A New Survey Shows; *Forbes,* June 21, 2019; https://www.forbes.com/sites/briannawiest/2019/06/21/a-new-study-shows-64-of-new-hires-will-leave-their-jobs-because-of-this-experience/#3626f06f247b.

Williams, Chris, Bridging the Communication Gap: How to Foster Effective Workplace Conversations, *Forbes,* August 9, 2023, https://www.forbes.com/sites/forbesbusinesscouncil/2023/08/09/bridging-the-communication-gap-how-to-foster-effective-workplace-conversations/?sh=4c0edba659a6

Yipa, Jeremy A., and Maurice Schweitzer, Losing your temper and your perspective: Anger reduces perspective-taking, *Organizational Behavior and Human Decision Processes,* January 2019.

Chapter 7

Abril, Danielle, Gen Z came to slay.' Their bosses don't know what that means, *Washington Post,* December 13, 2022, https://www.washingtonpost.com/technology/2022/12/12/gen-z-work-emojis/.

Bahr, Elisha, How to Retain Job Hoppers, December 3, 2015, https://www.clickboarding.com/the-3-best-ways-to-retain-job-hoppers/

BambooHR, Chapter 4: OnBoarding and Offboarding, *HR 101 Guide,* https://www.bamboohr.com/hr-101-guide/chapter-4-onboarding-and-offboarding.

BetterBuys, The Impact of Professional Development, https://www.betterbuys.com/lms/professional-development-impact/

Dewar, Carolyn, Scott Keller, Vikram Malhotra, and Kurt Strovink, Starting strong: Making your CEO transition a catalyst for renewal, November 17, 2022, *McKinsey Quarterly,* https://www.mckinsey.com/capabilities/strategy-and-corporate-finance/our-insights/starting-strong-making-your-ceo-transition-a-catalyst-for-renewal#/.

Eikenberg, Darcy, "Why your senior-level new hire isn't working out," Talent Management, September 11, 2023, https://www.talentmgt.com/articles/2023/09/11/why-your-senior-level-new-hire-isnt-working-out/.

Giulioni, Julie Winkle, *Promotions are SO Yesterday*, ATD Press (2022).

Hasl-Kelchner, Hanna. "Expert Background Check Basics Every Smart Employer Needs to Know," *Business Confidential Now with Hanna Hasl-Kelchner*. Podcast audio. October 20, 2016, https://businessconfidentialradio.com/expert-background-check-basics-every-smart-employer-need-to-know.

Hasl-Kelchner, Hanna. "How Encouraging Ambition Transforms Employees From Ordinary to Extraordinary," *Business Confidential Now with Hanna Hasl-Kelchner*. Podcast audio. January 6, 2022, https://businessconfidentialradio.com/how-encouraging-ambition-transforms-employees-from-ordinary-extraordinary.

Hasl-Kelchner, Hanna. "How to Guard Against a Toxic Workplace," *Business Confidential Now with Hanna Hasl-Kelchner*. Podcast audio. September 17, 2020, https://businessconfidentialradio.com/how-to-guard-against-toxic-workplace/.

Hasl-Kelchner, Hanna. "How to Improve Your Employee Orientation Process," *Business Confidential Now with Hanna Hasl-Kelchner*. Podcast audio. September 29, 2016, https://businessconfidentialradio.com/improve-employee-orientation-process/.

Hasl-Kelchner, Hanna. "How to Recruit the Right Talent in Today's Economy with Kathleen Quinn Votaw," *Business Confidential Now with Hanna Hasl-Kelchner*. Podcast audio. November 30, 2023; https://businessconfidentialradio.com/How-to-Recruit-the-Right-Talent-in-Todays-Economy-with-Kathleen-Quinn-Votaw.

Hasl-Kelchner, Hanna. "How to Surgically Hire and Fire to Get Your "Dream Team," *Business Confidential Now with Hanna Hasl-Kelchner*. Podcast audio. March 3, 2016, https://businessconfidentialradio.com/surgically-hire-fire-get-dream-team.

Hasl-Kelchner, Hanna. "Hire Higher: How To Hire A Dream Team With Andrea Hoffer," *Business Confidential Now with Hanna Hasl-Kelchner*. Podcast audio. November 17, 2022, https://businessconfidentialradio.com/hire-higher-how-to-hire-a-dream-team-with-andrea-hoffer/.

Hasl-Kelchner, Hanna. "What Every Responsible Leader Needs to Know About Pink-Collar Crime," *Business Confidential Now with Hanna Hasl-Kelchner*. Podcast audio. June 24, 2021, https://businessconfidentialradio.com/what-every-responsible-leader-needs-to-know-about-pink-collar-crime.

Hasl-Kelchner, Hanna. "Why Improving Franchise Growth is the Easiest Way to Unlock More Wealth," *Business Confidential Now with Hanna Hasl-Kelchner*. Podcast audio. September 2, 2021, https://businessconfidentialradio.com/why-improving-franchise-growth-easiest-way-unlock-more-wealth.

Hunter, Tatum, What's a scanner? GenZ is discovering workplace tech, *Washington Post*, March 8, 2023, https://www.washingtonpost.com/technology/2023/03/08/office-tech-young-old/.

Johnson, Cheryl, *Ambition: the Missing Attribute in Your Employees,* Cresting Wave Publishing (2019).

Kusy, Mitchell, *Why I Don't Work Here Anymore: A Leader's Guide to Offset the Financial and Emotional Costs of Toxic Employees,* CRC Press (2018).

Mitchell, Barbara and Cornelia Gamlem, *The Big Book of HR* (10th Anniversary Edition), Career Press, 2022.

Paxton, Kelly, *Embezzlement: How to Detect, Prevent, and Investigate Pink Collar Crime,* Independently Published (2020).

Rosner, Bob, and Allan Halcrow and Alan Levins, *The Boss's Survival Guide,* McGraw-Hill (2001).

Smith, Jacquelyn, 4 Common Reasons Half of All New Executives Fail, *World Economic Forum*, March 3, 2015, https://www.weforum.org/agenda/2015/03/4-common-reasons-half-of-all-new-executives-fail/.

University of Massachusetts, Business leaders explain how professional development benefits help with employee retention, https://www.umassglobal.edu/news-and-events/blog/professional-development-benefits.

Votaw, Kathleen Quinn, *Dare to Care in the Workplace: A Guide to the New Way We Work*, Advantage Media Group (2021).

Votaw, Kathleen Quinn, *Solve the People Puzzle: How High Growth Companies Attract and Retain Top Talent*, Advantage Media Group (2016).

Washington Post Live, Transcript: Anderson Cooper, CNN Anchor and Author, "Vanderbilt: The Rise and Fall of an American Dynasty." *Washington Post*, October 14, 2021, https://www.washingtonpost.com/washington-post-live/2021/10/14/transcript-anderson-cooper-cnn-anchor-author-vanderbilt-rise-fall-an-american-dynasty/.

Zara, Christopher, Your GenZ and millennial coworkers hate office jargon, so maybe avoid these 9 phrases, *Fast Company*, June 16, 2023, https://www.fastcompany.com/90911130/office-jargon-overused-annoying-gen-z-millennials-workplace-survey.

Chapter 8

Beemer, Jeffrey M., "Top 10 Mistakes to Avoid with Employee Handbooks," SHRM, November 13, 2015, https://www.shrm.org/resourcesandtools/legal-and-compliance/employment-law/pages/employee-handbook-mistakes.aspx.

Factorial, "Crafting an Employee Handbook: Tips, Advice and Best Practices," FactorialHR Blog, June 16, 2023, https://factorialhr.com/blog/employee-handbook/.

Forbes Human Resources Council, "15 Common Employee Handbook Mistakes To Avoid," *Forbes*, April 20, 2023, https://www.forbes.com/sites/forbeshumanresourcescouncil/2023/04/20/15-common-mistakes-to-avoid-when-creating-an-employee-handbook/?sh=6c23f7893eb6.

Hasl-Kelchner, Hanna. "Reduce Management Headaches with Proven Techniques to Better Manage Employee Expectations with Mimi Soule and Rob Wood," *Business Confidential Now with Hanna Hasl-Kelchner*. Podcast audio. October 5, 2023, https://businessconfidentialradio.com/Reduce-Management-Headaches-with-Proven-Techniques-to-Better-Manage-Employee-Expectations-with-Mimi-Soule-and-Rob-Wood.

Hasl-Kelchner, Hanna. *The Business Guide to Legal Literacy: What Every Manager Should Know About the Law,* Jossey-Bass, 2006.

Keches Law, "Can I Sue My Employer for Violating the Company Handbook?," Keches Law Group, December 1, 2016, https://kecheslaw.com/news/can-i-sue-my-employer-for-violating-the-company-handbook/#:~:text=This%20can%20be%20quite%20frustrating,violate%20their%20own%20handbook%20policies.

Mitchell, Barbara and Cornelia Gamlem, *The Big Book of HR* (10th Anniversary Edition), Career Press, 2022.

Sehra, Sabrina, How L&D teams should support the changing role of middle managers, Chief Learning Officer, November 28, 2022, https://www.chieflearningofficer.com/2022/11/28/how-ld-teams-should-support-the-changing-role-of-middle-managers.

Sember, Brette, "Employee Handbook Best Practices in 2023," *Forbes*, October 18, 2022, https://www.forbes.com/advisor/business/employee-handbook/

SESCO Management Consultants, "Avoid the Top 10 Mistakes in Employee Handbooks," https://sescomgt.com/resources/articles/avoid-the-top-10-mistakes-in-employee-handbooks/66

Silver, Melissa A., "5 Common Employee Handbook Mistakes and how to Fix Them," ALM BenefitsPro, January 31, 2022, https://www.benefitspro.com/2022/01/31/5-common-employee-handbook-mistakes-and-how-to-fix-them/?slreturn=20231104122336.

Epilogue

Simons, Daniel, *The Selective Attention Test*, YouTube, March 10, 2010, https://www.youtube.com/watch?v=vJG698U2Mvo

ACKNOWLEDGEMENTS

Books don't write themselves. It's a journey filled with speed bumps, detours, side trips, scenic overlooks, and lots of encouragement and help from individuals who believe in your message and the need to share it with the world. I'm therefore eternally grateful to the many talented people who have paved the way for the creation and publication of this book, especially:

Conni Francini, my editor whose valuable expertise in helping thought leaders refine their ideas helped me map out a more compelling way to convey my message;

Abby Greene, my dear friend and go-to graphic designer whose artistic skills enriched my text with visual elements and whose cover design brilliantly captured the hidden need for more fairness at work;

Courtney Kenney for her invaluable production support;

Tamela Rich, a cherished friend, accomplished author, editor, and traveler who inspired me to chart a new publication route;

Jess Todtfeld, a treasured media guru for his publicity insights and marketing assistance;

The wonderful guests I've been privileged to interview on Business Confidential Now who have selflessly shared their wisdom, including Jim Jeffers, Sarah Peyton, Scott Love, Kelly Waffle, Prof. Sim Sitkin, Warren Rustand, Dr. Diane Lennard, Ed Barks, Steven Howard, Dr. Kittie Watson, Sarita Maybin, Milo Shapiro, Anne Baum, Dr. Debra Dupree, Kathleen Quinn Votaw, Andrea Hoffer, Candice Tal, Kelly

Paxton, Julie Winkle Giulioni, Cheryl Johnson, Scott Greenberg, Rob Wood, Esq.; and Mimi Soule, Esq;

The encouragement of my friends at SCORE, especially Carl Baumann, Steve Fairchild, Abby Zarkin, and Marcia Ladd;

David H. Kelchner, my husband and love of my life, whose steadfast love and endless patience buoyed my writing journey,

And with the deepest gratitude and in loving memory of my parents, Gunda and Siegfried Hasl, whose unwavering support and moral compass has made everything possible.

Hasl
anno 1779

Hanna Hasl-Kelchner is a champion for fairness in the workplace. She helps organizations gain clarity to make more informed decisions by reducing complex concepts into sensible, bite-size pieces. Hanna accomplishes this as a business strategist and President of Business M.O., LLC; through her writing, speaking, consulting, and popular syndicated podcast, Business Confidential Now.

Hanna brings a unique perspective to the table, growing up in an entrepreneurial family and running a business before age 30 and blending it with decades practicing business law. Those experiences enabled her to successfully bridge the gap between the two disciplines during her career as a trusted advisor to influential decision makers ranging from startups to the S&P 500, Big Tobacco, and the White House. She has also had the privilege of being on the faculty at two top-ranked MBA programs: The Duke University Fuqua School of Management and the University of Virginia, Darden School of Business.

Hanna's first book, *The Business Guide to Legal Literacy* (Jossey-Bass, 2006), was an Amazon bestseller. Her articles have appeared in various print media and she's been a paid weekly contributor to Answers.com and AllBusiness.com. Hanna has also been quoted in the *Los Angeles Times, Bloomberg News,* and Society for Human Resources *HR Today Magazine* among others.

As a media source and acclaimed speaker, she has also appeared on radio and TV, including *Moving America Forward,* hosted by William Shatner. She was also filmed by Emmy Award-Winning Director and Producer Nic Nanton for a segment of *America's Premier Experts* that aired on ABC, NBC, CBS, and Fox affiliates nationwide.

Hanna is a proud member of the editorial board of *The Journal of Business Ethics Education,* having served since 2002, and as a certified mentor for SCORE (the nation's largest network of expert business mentors, a resource partner of the U.S. Small Business Administration) she received its highest honor (National SCORE Platinum Leadership Award) and the SCORE Chairman's Award.

Other accolades include being recognized by Dun and Bradstreet as a Twitter #BizInfluencer in the Specialty Strategy category (before Twitter became X) and called "a lawyer you can love" by a *Chicken Soup for the Soul* co-author.

Her formal education includes an undergraduate degree from Duke University, an MBA from Cornell University, and a JD from the Rutgers University School of Law.

Follow Hanna on LinkedIn, Twitter, and YouTube; through her websites (BusinessMO.com and SeekingFairnessAtWork.com); and podcast (*Business Confidential Now,* available wherever you get your podcasts and BusinessConfidentialRadio.com).

INDEX